TUCKER

TUCKER

CHADWICK MOORE

All Seasons Press

2881 E. Oakland Park Blvd. Suite 456

Fort Lauderdale, FL 33306

Edited by Harry Stein

Cover design by Mike Jackson, Beck & Stone

Interior design by Kim Hall

Note: QR codes link to interactive media referenced in corresponding chapter.

Library of Congress Cataloging-in-Publication Data has been applied for.

Hardcover ISBN: 978-1958682012

E-Book ISBN: 978-1958682029

Printed in the United States of America

10 9 8 7 6 5 4 3 2 1

TABLE OF CONTENTS

INTRODUCTION 1

PREFACE 9

CHAPTER ONE 13

CHAPTER TWO 23

CHAPTER THREE... 43

CHAPTER FOUR... 69

CHAPTER FIVE 75

CHAPTER SIX... 79

CHAPTER SEVEN 87

CHAPTER EIGHT 97

CHAPTER NINE.. 109

CHAPTER TEN 125

CHAPTER ELEVEN... 131

CHAPTER TWELVE 155

CHAPTER THIRTEEN... 163

CHAPTER FOURTEEN 185

CHAPTER FIFTEEN 197

CHAPTER SIXTEEN 203

CHAPTER SEVENTEEN.. 209

CHAPTER EIGHTEEN 213

CHAPTER NINETEEN 219

CHAPTER TWENTY.. 227

CHAPTER TWENTY-ONE 235

AFTERMATH 241

ACKNOWLEDGEMENTS 250

For Mia

INTRODUCTION

"Heard from everyone in the world today," a friend messaged me on April 24, 2023, as the news spread. "No one can believe it!"

"Tragic!" exclaimed another. "How could this happen?"

"What am I going to do with my evenings now?" wondered someone else.

You'd have thought Tucker Carlson had died.

And, indeed, for millions, on first hearing, that's how it felt. Over his seven years on Fox, Carlson had been not just a presence in our lives, but a source of nightly solace: someone who shared our horror and confusion about what was happening to the country we love and articulated it as no one else could, or dared to. Depressing as the intellectual and moral ruin in his accounting could sometimes be, his fierce independence of mind was always exhilarating. We knew we weren't alone.

His show was a ritual; people organized their lives around it.

So, yes, a death had occurred, but it wasn't Carlson's. Millions of populist civil libertarians were grieving because his erasure by Fox News signaled also our own silencing within mainstream media, which is to say, our participation in the national discourse.

"Tucker Carlson's firing puts the exclamation point on the recurring theme of his program," as Daniel J. Flynn put it in *The American Spectator*. "*Tucker Carlson Tonight* emphasized the ways in which the powerful few increasingly limited the choice of the faceless many. Whether discussing the Clinton campaign–bought Russian dossier used by the media and the Justice Department to undermine a duly elected president, the federal government's unconstitutional suppression of speech on social media, or a hundred other topics, Carlson took on bullies who wished to do an end-run on democracy."

"His enemies ironically proved through their heavy-handed approach his show's loose, ongoing thesis. They could not beat him in the ratings. They could only delete him from the TV listings."

Needless to say, the grim sorrow with which conservatives greeted the news was matched by exultation on the other side. For years, progressives — and more than a few mainstream Republicans — had portrayed Carlson as a figure of comic-book evil, a horrifying mix of right-wing Johnny Appleseed, calculatedly spreading pernicious disinformation among the great unwashed, and a media Darth Vader, his massive ratings seemingly lending him an air of indestructibility. Though most never watched his show, they had no doubt that even more than in other cases, all the usual epithets applied — racist, sexist, anti-Semite, homophobe.

For many Tucker fans, the crowing from the left was almost as hard to take as the news itself.

Alexandria Ocasio-Cortez all but took personal credit for Carlson's removal, glibly declaring "de-platforming works, and it is important and there you go." The doe-eyed authoritarian suburbanite appeared the day before on former Biden Press Secretary Jen Psaki's MSNBC show to call for a permanent federal ban on Carlson and his ilk. "We have very real issues with what is permissible on air. We saw that with January 6th and we saw that in the lead up to January 6th and how we navigate questions — not just of freedom of speech but also accountability for incitement of violence — this is the line that we have to really explore through law as well."

What's most stunning was the brazenness. A major network had caved to political and regulatory pressures, and the leftists behind it didn't even feel the need to pretend otherwise.

This is the way healthy societies die.

MSNBC, in its dance on Tucker's putative grave, lent new dimension to the concept of projection. "Carlson has demonstrated a gift for Fox's core constituency of keeping viewers from changing the channel by making them angry, aggrieved, and afraid," its hack finger-wagged, and he had sought to "maximize ratings by creating the most potent possible blend of demagoguery and resentment."

Jimmy Kimmel did a late-night riff belittling Carlson, noting he'd previously been fired by MSNBC and CNN, cracking he'd won the "EGOT of cable news."

For its part, *Politico* claimed that officials at the Department of Defense — a frequent Carlson target for its increasing interest in wokeness over military preparedness — took the news with "delight and outright glee." "Good riddance," one such official told the outlet.

Meanwhile, one Republican senator spoke to *The Hill* (anonymously, of course) to the effect that Tucker "wasn't troubled by whether something was true or not. He was mean, irresponsible, and dangerous."

On and on it went, even as the big question — Why? — went for the moment unanswered. Speculation ran in multiple directions. Tucker had become too independent — and dangerous — in some of his views, especially his opposition to the war in Ukraine and his challenge to the media narrative on January 6.

Or was it the emails uncovered during the disastrous, just-settled Dominion Voting Systems defamation lawsuit that had cost Fox

$787 million dollars, wherein Tucker had been revealed as having open contempt for company higher-ups, with one oft-cited message showing him referring to a senior Fox executive as a "cunt."

PJ Media speculated that perhaps it was Fox's risk-assessment committee that had "come down against Carlson. None of the 'suits' in the media management world are fully at home employing a talent with the irrepressible ability to commit to free speech. Especially if the talent says unpleasant truths regulators and the politically powerful in Washington don't want to hear."

Or maybe it was that Fox News boss Rupert Murdoch had begun to find Carlson's overt religiosity off-putting; indeed, as sources had it, he'd called off his latest engagement after fiancée Ann Leslie Smith referred to Tucker as "a messenger from God."

Whether that was precisely the case or not, for legions of Tucker's fans, Rupert Murdoch had been revealed as a ruthless, long-past-his-prime corporate autocrat, who in the end cared not at all about his audience. And his feckless billionaire children were even worse.

Robert F. Kennedy Jr., who the previous week had announced his Democratic presidential bid on Tucker's show, tweeted that Fox had folded before "the terrifying power of Big Pharma," noting "Carlson's breathtakingly courageous April 19 monologue broke TV's two biggest rules: Tucker told the truth about how greedy Pharma advertisers controlled TV news content and he lambasted obsequious newscasters for promoting jabs they knew to be lethal and worthless."

The Wall Street Journal, as close as there is to an official News Corp bible, offered a hit piece disguised as "explanation." "Tucker Carlson's Vulgar, Offensive Messages About Colleagues Helped Seal

His Fate at Fox News," declared the headline, although the report failed to produce any examples other than his savaging of the senior Fox executive by text.

And, too, inevitably, there was the claim that Tucker had created a hostile work environment. This one came in the form of a lawsuit by former booker Abby Grossberg, who had never so much as met Carlson in person but complained she felt "isolated, overworked, undervalued," on the show, notwithstanding her $145,000 yearly salary. Her allegations of sexism stemmed from staffers displaying pictures of House Speaker Nancy Pelosi in a plunging swimsuit; and her claim of anti-Semitism was based on a producer having put three inflatable Christmas trees in the office, including one next to her desk labeled "Hannukah bush."

In short, the lawsuit was itself evidence of precisely the intellectual and moral corruption Tucker nightly addressed on his show.

Nonetheless, Grossberg's grift was in predictably high demand, with outlets like MSNBC and PBS linking it to Tucker's ouster.

Whatever the case, what was clear and undeniable is that the move immediately impacted the company's bottom line. Overnight, Fox stock lost nearly one billion dollars in value.

And Newsmax — Fox's very junior competitor — saw the ratings for its primetime shows more than double that week.

It took a few days before something else began to sink in: That great as the shock had been, and keen as the immediate sense of loss was, this was not necessarily bad news, at least in the long term. That Tucker is a unique and invaluable figure in America's media and cultural landscape is almost universally acknowledged on the right.

Reports had it that he was already besieged by offers, some backed by very, *very* substantial resources.

Having come to know Tucker well in the course of researching this book, I saw firsthand the breadth of his interests, the range of his enthusiasms, the sheer likeability of the man; and, given the size and loyalty of his following, there was not a scintilla of doubt in my mind that he would continue to play an outsized role in the nation's future.

Indeed, in a media landscape transforming with dizzying speed, the Fox cable-news model in which I watched him operate over the past year already seems outdated, while the ways he might move forward and broaden his reach are limitless.

This book is the story of how Tucker came to be who he is, and hold the views he does, and otherwise become the spokesman for the tens of millions of Americans alarmed and confused at finding themselves outliers and outcasts in their own country. So it is also necessarily the story of holding firm to beliefs and values in the roughest of times.

Tucker is "not unemployed," as conservative provocateur Kurt Schlichter put it in *Townhall* early that fateful week, "he is unleashed. Fox may not think it needs Tucker — and that will remain to be seen — but Tucker certainly does not need Fox. Tucker is a conservative giant, with only Rush Limbaugh at all comparable in his standing within the conservative movement. The answer to the question 'What will Tucker do now' is the same answer as the answer to the question about what the 800-pound gorilla will do: 'Anything he wants.'"

Sure enough, a few days later he was back.

Sitting in the tiny Florida studio he'd used half the year for *Tucker Carlson Tonight*, he took to Twitter at 8:00 p.m., the exact moment that for so long he'd gone live on Fox.

"Good evening, it's Tucker Carlson," he began with his usual gusto and proceeded to deliver a message of resilience and hope.

"One of the first things you realize when you step outside the noise for a few days is how many genuinely nice people there are in this country: kind and decent people, people who really care about what's true, and a bunch of hilarious people, also, a lot of those. It's got to be the majority of the population, even now, so that's heartening. The other thing you notice when you take a little time off is how unbelievably stupid most of the debates you see on television are. They're completely irrelevant. They mean nothing. In five years, we won't even remember that we had them. Trust me, as someone who's participated. And yet, at the same time, and this is the amazing thing, the undeniably big topics, the ones that will define our future, get virtually no discussion at all. War, civil liberties, emerging science, demographic change, corporate power, natural resources. When was the last time you heard a legitimate debate about any of those issues? It's been a long time. Debates like that are not permitted in American media. Both political parties and their donors have reached consensus on what benefits them, and they actively collude to shut down any conversation about it. Suddenly the United States looks very much like a one-party state. That's a depressing realization, but it's not permanent. Our current orthodoxies won't last. They're brain-dead. Nobody actually believes them. Hardly anyone's life is improved by them. This moment is too inherently ridiculous to continue, and so it won't. The people in charge know this. That's why they're hysterical and aggressive. They're afraid. They've given up persuasion. They're resorting to force. But it won't work. When honest people say what's true, calmly and without embarrassment, they become powerful. At the same time, the liars who've been trying to silence them shrink and they become weaker. That's the iron law of the universe. True things prevail. Where can you still find Americans saying true things? There aren't many places left, but there are some, and that's enough. As long as you can hear the words, there is hope. See you soon."

Within an hour, the video generated three times more eyeballs than his Fox News program ever had. By the next morning, it had been seen by fifty-five million people.

PREFACE

On September 17, 2022, seven thousand bikers convened at the 99 Speedway in Stockton, California for the funeral of Ralph "Sonny" Barger. California authorities were tense, concerned the event "could turn dangerous." San Joaquin County Sheriff Pat Withrow told reporters his department had spent $400,000 in preparation, with more agencies, including the California Highway Patrol, doling out additional millions.

Barger, who'd died the previous June of throat cancer at eighty-three, had long been the patriarch of the notorious Hells Angels motorcycle club, the outlaw "Maximus leader," in the words of the legendary gonzo journalist Hunter S. Thompson. Yet there, among a ramble of swarthy men in leather vests, exposed torsos, tattoos, pointed beards, armpits, and faded denim, in a button-up, blue gingham shirt, chinos, and loafers with no socks, stood Tucker Carlson. He ascended the tiny stage flanked by canopy tents and a sound system.

"Maybe it's evidence of the fact that Carlson will show up to any big, likely-to-be-publicized event he's invited to speak at," one confused San Francisco journalist would write afterward. "Or it's evidence of the unholy alliance between Trump-y America, far-right militia groups, outlaw biker gangs, and the conservative media elite."

Of course, if it were evidence of anything, it was that the blinkered and sequestered coastal liberal elites continue to have no understanding of those who dare push against the prevailing orthodoxy, or of the sometimes-incongruent alliances that defiance can produce. And, if possible, they have even less understanding of the object of their incessant rage, the man who was Fox News's biggest prime-time star Carlson, his mug endlessly plastered on Twitter feeds of left-wing media watchdogs reacting to his latest monologue with predictable accusations of racism, sexism, and transphobia.

What's curious is that there's no mistaking who Carlson actually is, or what he is about. All they need to do is listen.

"I almost never come back because it makes me sad," he said now, looking over the mass of bikers, "and standing here with all of you reminds me of the state I grew up in. I haven't smelled cigarette smoke in the state of California in thirty years, and I'm just so grateful to smell it, so thank you — and I'm not joking at all — so thank you to those of you who are smoking and persisting. Thank you to those of you who are going to the Stockton gun show in two days. God bless. I can't believe they still exist. I can't believe this California still exists, and I'm just really happy to see that it does."

Though he never met Sonny Barger, continued Carlson, he'd learned of a letter Barger wrote to his wife and friends that included the words: "Stand tall. Stay loyal. Remain free. And always value honor."

"I thought to myself, if there is a phrase that sums up more perfectly what I want to be, what I aspire to be, and the kind of man I respect, I can't think of a phrase that sums it up more perfectly than that. And I thought *that* came from Sonny Barger, the famous outlaw biker, that every mom in my neighborhood was scared shitless of as a child. That's Sonny Barger's worldview? Why aren't we hearing that from the people who run the country? Why is it left to Sonny Barger to say 'Stand tall. Stay loyal. Remain free. And always value honor.' The President of the United States should be saying that every single morning as he salutes the flag, but only Sonny Barger is saying it. And I thought to myself, I want to pay tribute to the man who spoke those words, and when I was invited to this funeral, I cleared my schedule, and I thought I don't care how hard it is to get from Maine to Stockton, I'm going, and I'm here, and I'm honored to be here."

CHAPTER ONE

In February 2017, I was surprised to hear from a producer from *Tucker Carlson Tonight,* inviting me to appear on the show. At the time, my television *bona fides* were all but nonexistent. My only prior appearances were a brief daytime news hit on the Canadian Broadcasting Channel regarding a story I'd written for *The Advocate* on gay rights in Russia in the run-up to the 2014 Sochi Olympics and a Headline News interview a couple of years later to discuss the aftermath of the Islamic terrorist attack on Pulse nightclub in Orlando, Florida that left forty-nine dead.

More to the point, I was not especially political. Before the 2016 election season, I'd followed politics from the sidelines. I could barely name five professional pundits. The handful of times I'd gone to Washington, D.C., for work I couldn't get out fast enough. I was repulsed by most of the people I encountered. I looked down on them for their mix of pomposity and banality, their grotesque and twee sense of self-importance, their faux sincerity and insular geekiness.

So if you'd told me in the summer of 2016 that I'd soon become a periodic fixture on television, and on Fox News of all places, I would have laughed in your face.

How, then, did it happen? Simple — the weekend before, I'd written a piece in the *New York Post* under the headline "I'm a Gay New Yorker, and I'm Coming Out Conservative."

Naïve as it sounds now, I didn't think such a stance was especially daring or controversial. Lots of former Democrats were moving rightward at the time. Indeed, as I later wrote, I "never would have participated in the piece had everyone else around me not been so preoccupied with announcing their own politics. I did it for peace of mind. I wanted anyone who was listening to know: Just because I'm gay, live in New York, and work in media," I didn't want to be typecast. "This was America, after all. Don't we have the right to speak our minds and disagree?"

As I wrote in the *Post*: "It can seem like liberals are actually against free speech if it fails to conform with the way they think. And I don't want to be a part of that club anymore."

The article went viral, to my amusement, surprise, and trepidation. Overwhelmingly, the response was positive. My inbox was flooded with hundreds of emails from strangers across the country, welcoming me to the "big tent," a Reaganism I'd been unfamiliar with previously. If I was getting hate mail, I didn't notice, overwhelmed with messages of love and support.

"I'm a preacher in West Texas and although I don't understand your lifestyle, I love you and welcome to the big tent," read one such e-mail. "If you're ever near Midland our home is open to you."

"I didn't know there were other people like me, thank you," a gay man from Staten Island wrote in a raw, lengthy message I read lying in bed that night, one that brought a tear to my eye. (Years later, at a political function, he introduced himself and couldn't believe I still remembered his email).

The News Corp building is a fifty-one-story limestone-and-glass slab in midtown Manhattan built in the International Style. It sits among two identical skyscrapers, completed in 1973 as an expansion of nearby Rockefeller Center. A permanent, idling armada of black SUVs awaits Fox News hosts, guests, and executives parallel to a line of concrete barriers that march up Sixth Avenue and protect the small plaza before the entrance. Tourists spill over from Times Square one long block away, or Radio City Music Hall, across the street, where they may pause to take a photograph or glance with wonder and intimidation at the imposing structure, its electric-blue news ticker scrolling twenty-four hours a day around the façade, and the stately portraits of the familiar primetime personalities. There's a Chick-fil-A across the street, which seems deliberately placed, and if you turn the corner west onto Forty-Seventh Street, you'll be in the heart of the Diamond District, among a scurry of Orthodox Jewish men in black coats, tall hats, and long-curled sidelocks.

In addition to housing the main Fox News studios, the building is home to Dow Jones & Company, *The Wall Street Journal*, and the *New York Post*, all owned by News Corp. For liberals during the Trump years, 1211 Sixth Avenue represented America's switchboard of evil, and I wisecrackingly came to refer to it as the Death Star.

On my first visit to *Tucker Carlson Tonight*, I was sent to the cavernous studio D, on the first floor toward the back of the building, at the end of a hallway past a green room, a kitchenette, and a line of hair and makeup rooms. The interview was conducted remotely, with Carlson at the Fox News studio in Washington, D.C. There was a sound technician to microphone you up, a floating camera attached to a large mechanical arm operated by some unseen person, and a producer sitting off in the shadows. Usually, these hits were done on the fourth floor, in what's known at Fox as "the pods," a pair of tiny rooms, little more than closets, each with a chair, a monitor, a camera, a box of Kleenex, bottle of water, and a background screen projecting a familiar, for Fox viewers, gently waving blue stars-and-stripes motif.

Watching that interview today, I look dorky. My white dress shirt is a bit dingy and buttoned up too high. My eyes frequently drift to the monitor below the camera, watching myself, self-consciously. I fidget and bounce around in my seat too much as the camera tracks me as I speak. I look like a lot of first-timers do.

"Well, a gay journalist in Brooklyn has done just about the bravest thing a gay Brooklyn journalist can do," began Tucker's intro. "He abandoned trendy lifestyle liberalism for something else. Chadwick Moore wrote a pretty straightforward profile of Milo Yiannopoulos for a left-wing gay magazine last fall. The simple profile cost him many of his friends and triggered a wave, a big wave of online hostility. The backlash, Moore said in a piece in the *New York Post*, caused him to reevaluate his beliefs and he decided that modern liberalism is 'ugly, lockstep, incurious, and mean-spirited.'"

It's a surreal experience to go from just some guy, as I saw myself — whose whole life had been a series of shots in the dark, trial and error, bumbling toward varying successes and failures — to, in a split second, having millions of eyes on you.

"So," continued Carlson, "you found yourself looking at the community you live in through a very different lens all of a sudden, you wrote. And what did you see?"

"An aversion to communicating with people who don't agree with you and to understanding why exactly Trump became so popular and eventually won," I reply. "Um, and, and also now that the election is over, sort of evaluating how the Democratic Party and how the far left alienated so many people and how they messed up so badly. You know, I thought that after the election, they would have sat down and, you know, had a come, had a come-to-Jesus moment. And that hasn't happened at all."

"What an interesting journey you're on, Chadwick," Tucker concludes the interview moments later, "I hope you keep writing about this."

Something dissociative happens in those two-to-four-minute live-television hits. You get up from the chair in an adrenaline daze — *What just happened? What did I say?* — made stranger by how ordinary all this is to the people who work in television. I may have felt in those four minutes my life had changed forever, but for everyone else in that building and two hundred miles away in Washington, that's just Tuesday's C block and there's an assembly line of butts that need to get into that chair after you.

Still, for all that, something else about that first time at Fox News headquarters in 2017 left a huge impression: just how happy everyone seemed. I'd lived in New York for well over a decade, but I'd never been inside an office building in midtown Manhattan where everyone seemed so friendly, from the guy at the front desk, to the security guards, to the producer who met me at the door, and the technicians who miced me up and, especially, in the makeup chair.

That's where I met Vincenza, a vociferous and spritely Italian woman from the Bronx. "At Fox, we want everyone to look beautiful, liberal or conservative," she'd later remark to me. By the time she'd finished tending to my face with exacting, almost surreal, care and precision, we'd passed the time gossiping about celebrities, dishing about ex-boyfriends, and had exchanged phone numbers and Instagram handles. Compared to the gruff and bustle feet away on Sixth Avenue, inside Fox News felt more like a land of gumdrops and magical elves.

In the years since, I'd been there dozens of times and that never changed. Vincenza is no longer with the network, but I still looked forward to the makeup chair each time I went to Fox News. In the book *Roger Ailes: Off Camera,* author Zev Chafets recounts a story Ailes told him about a cleaning lady at Fox whom he noticed wearing a lot of makeup. Although Ailes's tenure at Fox ended badly, with bitterness, as he was tossed out — some would say smeared — as a sexual abuser, for decades he was a beloved and respected figure at the network he founded. In the anecdote, Ailes asked if the cleaning woman had a social event after work. A single mother from North Africa, the woman admitted she'd been in the makeup room giving herself the star treatment, and that it had always been her dream to be a beautician. Ailes, on the company dime, sent her to an expensive cosmetology school. "I had seen her around the office and noticed she was always in a good mood. That's critical for a makeup artist. They're the last ones the talent encounters before going on the air. If they are negative people, they can bring down the show," he told Chafets.

Was this normal for cable television? Apparently not. Some weeks later I was invited to audition to be part of a weekly panel on S.E. Cupp's new program, *Unfiltered*, on Headline News at the CNN building across town. The lobby was dim, chilling, stark, and bloodless. The receptionists were frigid, hurried, and condescending. Upstairs, in the makeup chair, a hobgoblin appeared to metastasize from thin air, waddled over, inspected my face, put a couple dabs of powder on my forehead, grunted, then motioned for me to get up and get out. Maybe at CNN, only the liberals got bronzer, lip gloss, brushed eyebrows, and delightful chit-chat.

The auditions weren't much better. The guests had nothing to say to each other during down time and sat in awkward, phone-scrolling silence. The hosts seemed disdainful toward those of us they didn't recognize from parties in the Hamptons and inside their corporate media fishbowl. At CNN, if you were a nobody, like me, you felt like one. After the second audition, I wasn't asked to come back, probably due to a remark I made about feminism that received a snarling glare from Cupp seated across the table.

The blowback that followed that first appearance on the Carlson show was instantaneous. Two days later, I was fired from my job as editor-at-large at the gay magazines *Out* and *The Advocate*, where my many cover stories included both the Pulse massacre and the dive into Russia's gay underbelly. Then *The Advocate* blocked me on social media.

This was a shock. At the time, I was barely living paycheck-to-paycheck, I had no savings, and I couldn't pay my bills. After several months, I was hauled into eviction court. My friends, all New York and London creative-class liberals and intelligentsia, soon abandoned me over my public political realignment. I started drinking too much.

Tucker's producers didn't know I was going through any of this, of course, nor did their boss. Still, when I kept getting invited onto the show, I couldn't quite figure out why. While on-air (and on social media) I cultivated a happy-warrior persona, I didn't feel I was particularly clever, and I certainly wasn't important. What had I accomplished compared to people who'd spent their entire lives analyzing politics and jostling for a few minutes of coveted airtime on cable news? I'd sometimes overhear them in the elevators or hallways of Fox News, talking heads talking to producers, with variations of the same question: *When are you going to have me back on?*

Gradually, as I came to better know him, I realized that for Carlson, that was probably part of my appeal. Even though I grew up far outside polite society, there's some inborn, WASP aversion to self-promotion within me. Maybe that's just a part of being from Appalachian stock.

Moreover, I do have strong convictions, and am not shy about expressing them. It's also the case that the scorned or disaffected liberal was a Tucker staple, not only on his show, but in his audience. While I may have been among the first to make a splash about it, an untold number of people left the Democratic Party in the years surrounding Donald Trump's election, some becoming high-profile figures, and they almost always had a spot on Tucker's show at the moment of their public excommunication from liberalism.

On one occasion, I sparked conversation with a woman sitting next to me in the green room at Fox. She was around my age, beautiful and sophisticated, with long, dark hair and dressed in black. She worked at a liberal magazine. She, too, was to be on Tucker's show that night. Earlier that day she'd been at the center of a Twitter firestorm after writing something perceived as a slight against transgender ideology — in the usual fashion, a simple defense of biological women. The mob came for her nonetheless, and she was invited on the show to explain what happened.

She'd never been on television, and she was nervous about that. But her biggest worry was that, like the mob earlier, Tucker would shred her. "I'm still a liberal," she said to me, "What do I do if he goes after me for my politics?"

I realized that, like most everyone in her circle, she didn't understand Tucker or his show. Finding myself in the role of prêt-à-porter seasoned TV professional, I told her several of his regular guests were self-identified liberals — the journalist Glenn Greenwald came to mind — and she was not in the crosshairs of a wicked force. Tucker is on your side here, I told her, no matter how you vote; what mattered is she didn't deserve the treatment she'd received over expressing a reasonable and sane opinion.

"If he asks something you're not prepared to answer, or don't want to answer, just politely pivot to something you do want to talk about," I told her. "He's not going to drill you. The goal is to keep the dialogue flowing."

She did a fine job; as I expected, it was a friendly and compassionate interview. I never saw her again, at Fox, or anywhere, and wondered if she left the media world and New York or, like so many others, had a taste of the consequences for wrongthink, begged for mercy and crawled back to her abusers. Maybe now she's banished somewhere to the far corners of a Condé Nast blog writing *House of Dragons* recaps, safely tucked away from the live wire of transgender theory.

Whatever the case, that night she learned what Tucker's viewers already knew. He is, above all, a person who hates hypocrisy and admires bravery. He regularly commented, unscripted, on his admiration for those who go against the grain and speak up in defense of what they believe, liberal or conservative or anything in between. The tagline of his show — "the sworn enemy of lying, pomposity, smugness, and groupthink" — hadn't come from nowhere. A civil libertarian himself, unlike most of us Tucker doesn't bat an eye at accusations of "racism" — a smear he faces daily, disseminated from America's most powerful and wealthy individuals and institutions. In fact, the allegation is hilarious to him. "The only people I actually hate are white liberals. It's people who look like me! Does that make me racist?" he would later tell me one night over dinner, followed by his characteristic, high-pitched, cutting chortle — an outburst delightful to both his viewers and anyone sitting around a dinner table with him.

Of course, my acquaintances on the left, in their debased view, assumed I was doing the show for the money. Inerudite, anonymous trolls found it a simple way to dismiss anything I said against the left: I'd sold out my community for a lucrative grift and all that "Fox News money." It was a darkly funny accusation as eviction papers were getting taped to my door. The fact is, after six years of appearing regularly on the network, I can report that, though occasionally enjoying a free cup of coffee or complimentary cookie in the green room, I'd been paid exactly zero dollars and zero cents by Fox News. The compensation was in the immovable conviction that everything I said was honest, and that I had done nothing wrong. In that sense, it was both the darkest and most important time of my life.

But of course, even at the worst of it, I was experiencing just the tiniest taste of what Carlson lives with every waking moment of his own life.

CHAPTER TWO

The village of Bryant Pond, population 1,300, sits in the rolling hills of western Maine, off Route 26. Also known as Lake Christopher, Bryant Pond is a spring-fed, two-mile long body of water in Oxford County straddled by the towns of Woodstock and Greenwood. Today, Oxford County has about 57,000 residents. Encompassing 2,176 square miles, or nearly twice the size of Rhode Island, Oxford County has a population density of about twenty-six people per square mile.

Bryant Pond is known for being the last place in America to get rid of hand-cranked telephones, only converting to dial phones in 1982. Before that year, phone calls were handled through a two-position magneto switchboard in the living room of the couple who owned the Bryant Pond Telephone Company. Today there's one mom-and-pop store and one motel in the town. A sawmill produced wooden clothespins in Bryant Pond until the 1970s. It used to be that the biggest thing to have ever come to town was the railroad, in 1851.

That was until one-hundred-sixty-nine years later, when Fox News set up shop there, in what was dubbed the network's "northernmost bureau."

Since childhood, Tucker Carlson has spent nearly every summer of his life in Bryant Pond, and he calls it his "favorite place in the world." He has plans eventually to retire there, and to spend eternity at Lakeside Cemetery next to the Universalist Church, established in 1843, where he has a plot.

"What's so evocative about the foliage in New England," he told me, "is that it dies every year. It comes in in May, and you enjoy it for three or four months. There's so much chlorophyll it's pulling the trees down. But then you're walking through the woods in the early fall, and suddenly you see red in the canopy, and, like, *what the fuck is that? Oh my gosh, they're dying already*. And there's this knowledge, this foreboding that it's all about to die . . . And so will I!" Carlson laughs. "The cycle of trees is the cycle of life. You can live in Florida and imagine it can go on forever, which is why old people move there — because they don't want to be reminded. But when you're in Maine, you know in late September that in three months it will be covered in snow and ice, and the bears will be hibernating, the animals will be in their little snow caves. Why would I want to miss that?"

Town Manager Vern Maxfield recalls seeing Tucker as a teenager around the village. "The Carlsons were just part of the summer guests at that time. They were respected and they just kind of fit in and became a part of the fabric of the town," he tells me. "He's very likable, very willing to stop and chat with you."

In December, 2018, when Carlson told Maxfield that he'd like to carve out a way to do broadcasts from the town so he wouldn't have to leave so often, Maxfield offered up the basement of the local Whitman Memorial Library, which is only open two days a week, and Carlson reportedly rented the ten-by-twenty-foot space for $2,500 a year. Soon after, he announced plans to buy the nearby town garage and convert it into a full-time studio, with room for a live audience.

Tucker's abiding affection for the town was not the only consideration behind the move. A month before he sent a letter to the town proposing the purchase of the property, Carlson's home in northwest Washington, D.C. was attacked by a mob of Antifa-linked radicals. It was November 7, 2018 — the day after the hotly-contested 2018 midterm elections. Carlson was at his desk in the Fox News bureau in Washington, preparing that evening's broadcast, when around 6:30 p.m. he started getting frantic texts from neighbors about a ruckus outside his home.

"I called my wife," Carlson told *The Washington Post* the next day. "She had been in the kitchen alone getting ready to go to dinner and she heard pounding on the front door and screaming. . . . Someone started throwing himself against the front door and actually cracked the front door." Carlson's four children were not home at the time. According to a police report, Carlson's wife Susie "retreated to a room in the rear of her home" after the attack began.

According to reports, the swarm of about twenty self-described "anti-fascists" had blocked off both ends of Carlson's street, and carrying signs listing his address approached the house after dark. Video of the incident shows the group chanting "We know where you sleep at night," with some calling the television host "racist" and accusing him of "promoting hate."

"Tucker Carlson, we are outside your home," shouts one demonstrator in the video, apparently unaware that his show was scheduled to go live in an hour, so he'd likely be at work. Another woman is overheard saying she wanted to "bring a pipe bomb" to the demonstration. The crowd dispersed before police arrived, leaving behind an anarchist symbol spray-painted on the driveway. No arrests were made, despite police insisting the attack would be investigated as a hate crime of "anti-political bias."

According to *The Washington Post*, a member of the mob said the group "did not plan to protest in front of Carlson's home in the dark, but failed to account for last weekend's daylight saving time change." He added, "The reason for this tactic is to bring the pain that is felt every day among marginalized people who have been victims of right-wing politics to Tucker and make it personal. He has explicitly made far-right politics go mainstream. That is what he has done with his television show and platform."

"It wasn't a protest. It was a threat," Carlson told the *Post*. "They weren't protesting anything specific that I had said. They weren't asking me to change anything. They weren't protesting a policy or advocating for legislation. . . . They were threatening me and my family and telling me to leave my home."

In the aftermath of the event, the self-described "anti-fascists," calling themselves Smash Racism DC, were unrepentant and boastful. "Tonight you're reminded that we have a voice," they tweeted. "Tonight, we remind you that you are not safe either," claiming that Carlson spread "fear into our homes" nightly via the television. The following day, on Facebook, they added: "Fascists are vulnerable. Confront them at their homes!" The account also shared Carlson's home address, as well as the home addresses of Carlson's brother and Carlson's friend Neil Patel, with whom he'd founded the conservative news site the *Daily Caller*.

Since the election of Donald Trump, such threats — and occasional outright attacks — on conservative notables had of course increased exponentially, urged on without consequence by major political and cultural figures on the left and their allies in the media. leftists openly organized on social media platforms like Twitter and Facebook to dox, stalk, harass, and threaten prominent conservatives around Washington, D.C.

The previous June, California congresswoman Maxine Waters had infamously ranted to a crowd in Los Angeles that if they encountered Republican Members of Congress or Trump administration officials "in a restaurant, in a department store, in a gasoline station, you get out and you create a crowd, and you push back on them, and you tell them they're not welcome."

New Jersey Senator Cory Booker urged activists at one event, "Please don't just come here today and then go home. . . . Go to the Hill today. Get up and, please, get up in the face of some congresspeople."

Democratic National Committee deputy chair and Minnesota congressman Keith Ellison posted a photo on Twitter posing with a book called *Antifa: The Anti-Fascist Handbook*, which openly calls for violence while conducting "anti-fascist activity."

Meanwhile, soon-to-be reinstated Speaker of the House Nancy Pelosi's "I just don't even know why there aren't uprisings all over the country. Maybe there will be" was enthusiastically echoed by Hillary Clinton on CNN. "You cannot be civil with a political party that wants to destroy what you stand for, what you care about," declared the former First Lady, senator, and Democratic Party standard-bearer.

From the cultural left, the calls for outright violence were even more blatant. Comedian Kathy Griffin posed holding a bloody, severed head in the likeness of Donald Trump; the rapper Snoop Dogg released a music video portraying the murder of the forty-fifth president; and in a Public Theater production of Shakespeare's Julius Caesar in New York, the title character, depicted as a near-double for Donald Trump, was stabbed to death on stage. "I have thought an awful lot about blowing up the White House," Madonna proclaimed at a rally in Washington, D.C., and at the Glastonbury Festival in England, Johnny Depp, referencing the killing of Abraham Lincoln, asked an audience, "When was the last time an actor assassinated a president? It has been a while and maybe it is time."

Hardly incidentally, Depp's "joke" came a mere eight days after an armed attack on a group of Republican congressmen on a softball field in Alexandria, Virginia, left Republican majority whip Steve Scalise gravely wounded and five others hospitalized. The shooter, sixty-six-year-old James Hodgkinson, was a former Bernie Sanders campaign staffer who belonged to several political groups on Facebook with names like "Terminate the Republican Party," "The Road To Hell Is Paved With Republicans," and "Donald Trump is not my President."

In the run-up to the mob assault on Tucker's home, activists in D.C. had for weeks been angrily — and often illegally — pro-testing the nomination of Brett Kavanaugh to the Supreme Court. On September 24, hundreds stormed the U.S. Capitol complex, first targeting the offices of Republican senators Susan Collins of Maine and Jeff Flake of Arizona. They eventually took over the rotunda in the Russell Senate Office building, leading to the arrest of 128 people. Two weeks later, on October 6, dozens of left-wing activists pushed through a police line and stormed the steps of the Supreme Court building with raised fists, then banged on the doors attempting to break in.

The unlawful demonstrations, as well as the doxxing of conservative figures' exact whereabouts and home addresses were conducted in real time, publicly, on social media platforms like Twitter and Facebook — an obvious Terms of Service violation to which the tech giants turned a blind eye, though this is what enabled demonstrators to disrupt the lives of administration figures like Homeland Security Secretary Kirstjen Nielsen, advisor Stephen Miller, and former press secretary Sarah Huckabee Sanders, among others, when they ventured to Washington-area restaurants. "How can you sleep at night?" chanted activists, menacing Senate Majority Leader Mitch McConnell and his wife, Trump's Secretary of Transportation Elaine Chao, as they left an event in Georgetown.

Yet there was no one the mob despised more than Tucker Carlson — and no one more viciously targeted. Indeed, what he said every weekday night made him a pariah even in his own affluent Washington neighborhood. Over 90 percent of D.C. went for Hillary Clinton in 2016, compared to 85 percent of voters in San Francisco; 79 percent in New York City; 74 percent in Chicago; and 71 percent in Los Angeles County. In 2020, a mere 5 percent of Washington, D.C., would vote for Donald Trump.

As Carlson later put it on his Fox Nation show, *Tucker Carlson Today*: "There are 435 members of the House of Representatives, and if you lived in Washington, D.C., for the last thirty-five years — from say 1985 to 2020, as some of us have — you end up meeting a lot of them. And some of them are fine, but overwhelmingly they are hollow people who are in the business because they yearn for the affirmation of strangers, which is inherently sick. Who cares what strangers think of you? You should care what the people around you think of you, and you should do your best to treat them well. It's a basic life rule, but they ignore it. That's why they're politicians, because they're screwed-up people."

As observes one former, longtime Carlson neighbor — a conservative herself, she chooses to remain anonymous — Washington is "a very small town," with all that implies.

And when it comes to politics, it's more akin to Peyton Place than Mayberry. Impressive as it may be for visitors to walk through the nation's capital, admiring the imposing buildings and finding themselves moved to be at the site of so many stirring events, for many of those permanently ensconced in the place, the attraction lies less in reverence for history than in the lust for power and the proximity to it. With its tidal ebb and flow of politicians and their staffs lapping ashore and retreating every few years, it's an even smaller town for what some call "permanent Washington," the paper-pushers, bureaucrats, judges, and spies — and arguably even more of a snakepit.

Carlson's upscale neighborhood was home to the permanent elite class, including more than a few journalists, and the area is especially adamant in its ideological passions and resentments. Pre-Trump, says the neighbor, Tucker's contempt for liberal orthodoxy was easier to overlook; for all their ideological differences, after all, they still belonged to the same social set, went to the same parties, vacationed at the same places. But with Trump's election, Tucker "became kind of a pariah here even among people that were his lifelong friends. . . . In the last five years, he became a traitor to his class. . . . I suspect Tucker couldn't have done his show the same way if his kids had still been in school." She pauses. "I mean, he had to move out of D.C., he had to sell his house."

An incident on October 13, 2018, three weeks before the Antifa attack on his home, is especially telling. Carlson was dining at the Farmington Country Club in Charlottesville, Virginia, with his son, a student in the area, his nineteen-year-old daughter, and some family friends. According to Carlson, toward the end of the meal, on her way back from the bathroom and passing through the bar area of the club, his daughter was accosted by a man sitting at the bar. "A middle-aged man stopped my daughter and asked if she was sitting with Tucker Carlson. My daughter had never seen the man before. She answered: 'That's my dad,' and pointed to me. The man responded, 'Are you Tucker's whore?' He then called her a 'fucking cunt.' My daughter returned to the table in tears. She soon left the table and the club. My son, who is also a student, went into the bar to confront the man. I followed. My son asked the man if he'd called his sister a 'whore' and a 'cunt.' The man admitted he had, and again became profane. My son threw a glass of red wine in the man's face and told him to leave the bar, which he soon did.'"

Carlson complained to the club's management, which investigated the incident and eventually revoked the membership of the man, an artist named Juan Manuel Granados who splits his time between Florida and Virginia. His website reads: "After long carer [sic] in Advertising [sic] in Buenos Aires and NYC with multiple professional awards. [sic] Juan has been a full time Visual Artist [sic] for the last 10 years and has held multiple group and individual shows. Juan is and [sic] American citizen reside [sic] in Miami FL [sic] and Charlottesville VA [sic]."

Granados, a gay man, also sat on the board of a nonprofit called The Women's Initiative, which seeks to "provide women with effective counseling, social support and education so they can transform life challenges into positive change and growth," according to the group's website.

Many on the left reflexively took Granados's side. Headlines falsely claimed Carlson had assaulted the man in a homophobic, anti-immigrant attack, despite a video of the dustup circulating on social media showing Carlson, though using some profanity, as clearly calm and restrained. In a later statement, he said: "I love my children. It took enormous self-control not to beat the man with a chair, which is what I wanted to do. I think any father can understand the over-whelming rage and shock that I felt seeing my teenage daughter attacked by a stranger. But I restrained myself. I did not assault this man, and neither did my son. That is a lie. Nor did I know the man was gay or Latino, not that it would have mattered. What happened on October 13 has nothing to do with identity politics. It was a grotesque violation of decency. I've never seen anything like it in my life."

Michael Avenatti — the attorney who'd represented porn star Stormy Daniels in her lawsuit against then-president Donald Trump, and was known to Carlson's viewers as Creepy Porn Lawyer, or CPL for short — claimed he would be representing Granados in a lawsuit against Carlson. "You committed assault (learn the difference)," he wrote on Twitter. "Your friend committed assault . . . and battery (on video). You are the aggressor in the video as is your friend. The man at the bar sits there calmly. Numerous witnesses contradict your claim of innocence. Your daughter was drinking underage in a bar with your assistance and knowledge. You were intoxicated."

Creepy Porn Lawyer called his "client," Granados, "a leader in the community who has a history of standing up for what is right" and claimed Carlson "told the man to 'go back where you came from' before the video starts."

The lawsuit never materialized. In short order, Creepy Porn Lawyer was convicted of attempting to extort $25 million from athletic apparel company Nike and, in separate trials, of fraud and embezzlement from numerous clients, including Daniels. Once touted by left-wing media figures as a potential 2020 Democratic presidential candidate, he is currently serving a five-year sentence in prison.

Needless to say, those who took Granados's side in the ugly incident involving the Carlsons never issued an apology.

For those who know Carlson well, the left's stock characterizations of him register as bizarre. "Tucker's a racist?" says his father Dick, himself a former journalist, incredulously. "There's *no one* who takes people more as individuals. When his brother sees someone write that, he wants to go punch the guy out, but I just ask: 'What's the *matter* with them?' Because it's so far off, it's actually a psychological problem, this intense hatred. And I think what bothers them most is he's so sure of himself, he honestly doesn't *care* what they think."

When his sons were growing up, Dick Carlson was the epitome of a hands-off parent, but he says that seeing the virulence of the hatred Tucker faces today, "I always worry about him. It's hard to believe someone may take a shot at him, but I read these awful things and I do believe it. But he just ignores it, and plows forward."

Indeed, while of course keenly aware he is a potential target, Tucker himself doesn't dwell on it. "I'm not too worried in the same way I'm not worried flying through turbulence," he tells me. "You can't control it. If someone wanted to shoot me, he could. I hope nobody does. But I can definitely think of worse things than being assassinated — like humiliating myself, being caught lying, diminishing myself, embarrassing my children. I'm a fatalist. I'm going to be fifty-four. My kids are grown and they're great, I'm close to all of them. I've had an unusually happy marriage. I don't want to die, I don't have a death wish. But the whole idea that living as long as you can is the whole point of life is ridiculous to me. What matters is how you live."

On November 8, 2018, the day after the attack on Carlson's home and in a seemingly quiet protest of the platform's double standards for content moderation, the official Fox News Twitter account, with over 20 million followers, went dark. Fox News would not tweet again for nearly a year and a half, only resuming use of the service on March 18, 2020. The first tweet back related to the novel Covid-19 pandemic: "Keep up with all the latest COVID-19 news, including tips on keeping safe and stories of survival, struggle and inspiration, at Foxnews.com," it read.

"We intentionally moved out of D.C. to Maine and Florida, where I can walk the beach and pray and we can be in the woods," Tucker's wife Susie later tells me. "It's all about trying to orient your daily life, too. Prayer and finding peace, so that you are intentional about creating a world where that is easier to do and there's less noise."

However, having played no small part in running Carlson out of Washington, D.C., *The New York Times* soon followed the cable host to Maine. On July 20, 2020, Carlson disclosed to his millions of viewers that a reporter for the paper was planning to expose his new address. "They hate my politics. They want this show off the air," he said on that night's broadcast. "If one of my children gets hurt because of a story they wrote, they won't consider it collateral damage. They know it's the whole point of the exercise: to inflict pain on our family, to terrorize us, to control what we say. That's the kind of people they are."

Citing the events outside his home in Washington, Carlson added, "their story about where we live is slated to run in the paper this week. Editors there know exactly what will happen to my family when it does run."

The paper swiftly denied the accusations. "While we do not confirm what may or may not publish in future editions," a spokesperson told *The Washington Post*, "the *Times* has not and does not plan to expose any residence of Tucker Carlson's, which Carlson was aware of before tonight's broadcast."

Carlson's strategy to get ahead of the report appeared to work; the story never ran. Only two years later, in a three-part, front-page hit piece devoted to Carlson written by MSNBC contributor Nicholas Confessore, did the *Times* casually acknowledge it had indeed planned to dox Carlson, writing, "Mr. Carlson would raise the stakes when The *Times* later assigned a freelancer to write about his life in Bryant Pond, accusing the paper of seeking to endanger his wife and children."

In his letter to the town of Bryant Pond, Carlson had offered to buy the unused town garage and parking lot for $30,000. The building had originally been a horse stable for patrons of the nearby, now abandoned, Grange Hall, a meeting spot for a fraternal organization dedicated to agricultural advocacy founded after the Civil War. Carlson laid out his intention to repair the property and install an advanced TV studio.

But several months later Carlson was forced to scrap the plan when the local Lewiston *Sun Journal* newspaper published a piece highly critical of both the move and Carlson himself. Written by a local reporter named Steve Collins, it was littered with petty slights, and went out of its way to paint Carlson as a faux-Mainer. It called Carlson politically "off-the-wall" and noted that Carlson "has occasionally shown some specific knowledge of the area, though not always accurately. For example, three years ago, Carlson talked about the Somali community in Lewiston, claiming 'the left moved thousands' of refugees from camps in Kenya to Maine, a misleading summary. The early immigrants moved on their own to Lewiston from Atlanta, where they had been settled." Regarding the upcoming annual town meeting to decide the future of the property, the reporter sniped: "Carlson, who can't vote because he's only a part-time resident, is not expected to show up."

Anticipating the piece would provoke a strong reaction locally, Carlson expected it would kill the deal. "I can't have the building now," he said with evident regret, noting that Fox would surely be hesitant to invest a million dollars' worth of equipment in a tiny, rural studio whose presence and location would now be widely known. "I'm kind of crushed" and "kind of bitter about it," he said, calling the report a "total violation of my privacy."

Steve Collins, for his part, gloated on Twitter. "Sorry, Bryant Pond, but @TuckerCarlson is pulling the plug on his proposal for a

Fox News studio in the old town garage. He told me my 'hit piece' made the project impossible."

A vote on the matter was held anyway, in late March, and the townspeople unanimously voted to allow Carlson to purchase the old garage and set up a base in Bryant Pond, whether he still wanted it or not. He bought the property that fall, laying out plans, according to town records, to invest $88,000 to repair and upgrade the building while retaining its original look and character.

There's no stoplight on the stretch of Route 26 where, since 2019, the most influential cable news show in American history broadcast for at least half the year. Nestled as it is among a tiny outcrop of quiet buildings on the side of the road, in fact there's no indication that a television studio sits here at all.

"I don't see that it's changed the community at all," Town Manager Vern Maxfield tells me. "It's very quiet. His guests come and go. I find that a lot of local people don't realize he's here — people are often surprised when they find out. Otherwise, he's just very much welcome and part of the community.

"It's neat to say, when I'm watching his show, I know right where he's sitting, I've been in that studio, and it's being broadcast all over the world," adds Maxfield, who's been Town Manager for over thirty years. "That's exciting to me. It's totally amazing."

A man in blue jeans, T-shirt, wrap-around sunglasses, and a low-slung camo baseball cap leans against a parked car outside the former garage as we pull into the gravel driveway. He's silent as the eastern white pines as he moseys over to the car window to check our credentials — Carlson's security guard, I presume — before nodding that we are cleared to proceed. Inside, another local man — greasy dark hair snaking from beneath a stained baseball cap, a few missing teeth, blue jeans, and firearm on his hip — preps dinner. This is Sherwood, the cook, one of two Sherwoods who works for Carlson in Maine. His wife does hair and makeup for the show.

It's a Tuesday and Carlson is finishing up that night's live broadcast in a room to the right. Steak with potatoes is on the menu for him and his guests, who include journalist Chris Bray, former Canadian NHL hockey star and Olympic gold medalist Theo Fleury, and me.

Shortly after nine o'clock, Carlson bursts into the main room and offers us something to drink — beer, soda, sparkling water. Bray takes a beer, the rest of us sparkling water. "Are we all on the Perrier plan?" Carlson asks, tickled, a reference to his over twenty years of sobriety.

That's one thing you immediately notice about Carlson; he has the sort of corybantic energy often found in teetotalers, a sort of hyperactive acuity to the present that would be familiar to those who've spent time around such people even if he didn't occasionally reference his sobriety. He's animated. He flaunts an intense enthusiasm for those around him but in a way that doesn't cajole. It's a manner the chemically reliant can find distressing; for people who always need something to take the edge off, it's a little too sharp and a bit too present.

Temptation is not a problem for Carlson. There's alcohol all around his houses; here there's a fridge stocked with beer, a full bar in the dining room. He also makes a habit of hiring people who've been to rehab — groundskeepers, caretakers, and security staff.

"I thank God I've always been one of those people who's really grateful to be sober. I never have felt like, 'Oh man, I miss it,'" Carlson later tells me.

The garage in Maine is a wonderland of curiosities. Bookshelves line the two longer walls of the rectangular space that has been refurbished in floor-to-ceiling natural pine. Between them are a wooden bar, an open kitchen, a sitting area, and two long dining tables that serve as work stations for the show's small, on-site staff. One of his producers, Charlie, enjoys Maine so much he permanently relocated to Oxford County and stays even over the winter months, when Carlson and his wife decamp to Florida and Tucker does the show from there. During his first season up north, Charlie stayed in one of Carlson's fishing shacks that didn't have electricity or plumbing. He loved that, too.

Above one table in the studio, on a wooden trellis that looks like it was part of the original construction, dangles the skin of a mountain lion. Above the other table is a chandelier made of antlers. There are skulls of various critters, a three-foot-long turtle shell, a patinated statue of the Madonna with child, old newspapers in frames ("WE DROP ATOM BOMB ON JAPS," reads one front page), oil paintings, urns, an antique model passenger-liner, tusks, and other rustic bric-a-brac. It is the den of an inquisitive, which is to say literary, man.

And that Tucker very much is. He doesn't get enough credit for being an extremely skilled writer. In that sense, his appeal goes beyond politics. As a former liberal-arts major and once aspiring fiction writer, I've always seen Carlson as belletristic in a way few talk-show hosts ever have been. That's especially evident in his opening monologues, which were so vivid in their characterization of the state of American life and culture they sent millions of viewers off to bed with depressive foreboding.

Next to a portrait of a cocker spaniel hangs a letter-sized black-and-white caricature of Carlson and Hunter S. Thompson, the founder of so-called gonzo journalism, who arguably had a greater impact on the young Tucker than any other writer. The two are seated at a round dinner table beaming at one another. Thompson, with a cigarette dangling from his mouth, is shaking Carlson's hand with the other on his shoulder.

Himself a legendary abuser of alcohol, as well as pretty much every drug that passed his way, Thompson committed suicide in 2005 at the age of sixty-seven. He initially came to prominence in 1967 with the publication of *Hell's Angels*, for which he spent a year riding with the motorcycle club documenting their lives — and which surely had something to do with Carlson's showing up unexpectedly to Sonny Barger's funeral.

In 1981, when Carlson was twelve, a guest in the Carlson home left behind a copy of Thompson's most famous book, *Fear and Loathing in Las Vegas*. "I liked the cover art, so I read it. It changed my life," Carlson wrote in *The Weekly Standard* weeks after Thompson's suicide.

"The book made me want to drop everything (specifically, the sixth grade) and take up journalism. It made me want to travel the world with a pen and notebook, having adventures, recording my observations, and speaking fearlessly on behalf of truth as a sworn guardian of the First Amendment."

In 1958, Thompson, just out of the Air Force, penniless, and living in New York City, wrote on a job application for the *Vancouver Sun*: "As far as I'm concerned, it's a damned shame that a field as potentially dynamic and vital as journalism should be overrun with dullards, bums, and hacks, hag-ridden with myopia, apathy, and complacence, and generally stuck in a bog of stagnant mediocrity."

Thompson didn't get the job, but his disdain for American journalism and political orthodoxy remained foundational throughout his career. "The most consistent and ultimately damaging failure of political journalism in America has its roots in the clubby/cocktail personal relationships that inevitably develop between politicians and journalists," he wrote in *Fear and Loathing on the Campaign Trail '72*. "Absolute truth is a very rare and dangerous commodity in the context of professional journalism," he wrote in another essay that year.

In his 1988 book *Generation of Swine*, a collection of writings from his *San Francisco Examiner* column, Thompson wrote of the rise of cable and satellite television: "The TV business is uglier than most things. It is normally perceived as some kind of cruel and shallow money trench through the heart of the journalism industry, a long plastic hallway where thieves and pimps run free and good men die like dogs, for no good reason."

In that same book, he observed of the 1980s: "There are times, however, and this is one of them, when even being right feels wrong. What do you say, for instance, about a generation that has been taught that rain is poison and sex is death? If making love might be fatal and if a cool spring breeze on any summer afternoon can turn a crystal blue lake into a puddle of black poison right in front of your eyes, there is not much left except TV and relentless masturbation. It's a strange world. Some people get rich and others eat shit and die."

For Carlson's viewers, this veneration of the bucolic over a toxic, electrified derangement infecting a world dominated by mass media will have a very familiar ring.

The year Thompson published *Generation of Swine*, Carlson, then an eighteen-year-old college freshman, drove to Providence, Rhode Island, to see Thompson debate G. Gordon Liddy at Brown University.

"Thompson showed up slobbering, then got even drunker. He took swigs from a bottle of whiskey and yelled incoherently about Richard Nixon. But booze wasn't the basic problem. Dead sober, Thompson still would have embarrassed himself. He didn't have much to say. Later I learned that every childhood hero disappoints you if you get close enough. But that night at Brown, I was stunned, and totally disillusioned. Thompson wasn't anything like I'd imagined," Carlson wrote.

Eighteen years later, and just a month before Thompson's suicide, Carlson had the opportunity to meet the man. A friend invited him to dinner with Thompson in New Orleans. "We met at Arnaud's in the French Quarter. Thompson couldn't make it to the second floor dining room because of a bad leg, so we sat at the bar. He didn't say much, and when he did he spoke in a faint, slurry voice. He smiled a lot. He could not have been nicer. I wasn't shocked this time, just sad. For a while, Thompson was the funniest writer in America. His sentences were tight and precise and perfectly balanced. Now he seemed almost unable to communicate with words. After an hour or so, I got up to leave. Rather than shake my hand, Thompson leaned forward and pulled me in, hugging me so hard and for so long that his lapel pin left an imprint on my cheek," Carlson wrote. "Then he handed me his pack of Dunhills, Superior Mild, with one left in the box."

Carlson has held on to it ever since. The pack of Dunhills sits inside his desk drawer in Maine, as a relic.

CHAPTER THREE

No one in American public life today, aside perhaps from those in religious leadership (and precious few of them), speaks so passionately or so often about the vital importance of family and children to personal and societal well-being than does Tucker Carlson, or warns more ominously of the threat of civilizational collapse — nihilism, broken homes, a decayed social fabric — posed by the ever more audacious anti-family excesses of modern secular society.

"When I hear people say abortion is the most important right that we have, I ask myself, what are you really saying?" as he put it in September 2022, addressing the audience at the Family Leadership Summit in Des Moines, Iowa.

"We need to take three steps back and ask ourselves, what is this exactly? What are they promising the American population when they promote this? Of course, what they're saying — and what Citi Bank and Nike and Dick's Sporting Goods and all these huge companies that are affirmatively promoting abortion by paying their female employees to have abortions — they're really saying it's more important to serve us than to have a family. You'll be happier as you rise within our company than if you had your own children. I never hear any Republican pushback against this, but I cannot imagine a more grotesque and obvious lie. But it doesn't detract from the unchangeable fact that children are the main source of joy and meaning in the human life. Anyone who tells you: no, what you really want, Miss Twenty-eight-year-old CitiBank Employee, is to move up to assistant vice president in charge of international bonds. Really? Is someone from the HR department going to hold my hand in hospice, forty years from now? Is the company going to love me unconditionally? No, it's a lie. And by telling that lie they are stripping young Americans of the promise of the only thing that matters, which is having a family."

Obviously, as his many, many disquisitions on the subject make clear, Carlson is well prepared to make this case on an intellectual basis. But just as obviously, it is something he feels to the very depth of his being, and is reflected in the way he orders his existence. It is no exaggeration to say that his conviction about the centrality of family to the properly lived life are key to his emotional DNA.

That we live in a culture where children increasingly pay the price for the self-indulgent narcissism of their elders in neglect and abandonment is for Carlson not an abstraction; it has resonance in his own family, echoing down through the generations.

Tucker McNear Carlson was born in the Mission District of San Francisco on May 16, 1969. Richard Nixon, elected by the so-called Silent Majority, was four months into his presidency. The Summer of

Love had ended two years earlier, and three months later the Manson murders would horrify the nation.

Already a backlash against the excesses of the hippie counterculture was brewing across America.

Author Joan Didion famously documented the underbelly of the hippie phenomenon on a 1967 reporting trip to San Francisco. Far from the peace, love, and daisy chains version of the late sixties of baby boomer nostalgia, the America Didion wrote of was a nation in deep moral crisis, one that would be recognizable fifty years later in a *Tucker Carlson Tonight* monologue.

As she put it in her 1968 classic *Slouching Towards Bethlehem*, "It was a country of bankruptcy notices and public-auction announcements and commonplace reports of casual killings and misplaced children and abandoned homes and vandals who misspelled even the four-letter words they scrawled."

"It was a country in which families routinely disappeared, trailing bad checks and repossession papers. Adolescents drifted from city to torn city, sloughing off both the past and the future as snakes shed their skins, children who were never taught and would never now learn the games that had held the society together.

"It was the United States of America in the year 1967. . . . All that seemed clear was that at some point we had aborted ourselves and butchered the job," she wrote.

And San Francisco was ground zero. The City by the Bay "was where the social hemorrhaging was showing up. San Francisco was where the missing children were gathering and calling themselves 'hippies.'"

The fact of being born in this place, at this time, would have immense consequences in young Carlson's life, not least in how he thinks about America all these years later.

Carlson's own father was an orphan. His birth mother was one of the children of privilege who rushed headlong into California's counterculture, in her case abandoning her husband of seven years and two young children.

Born June 4, 1945 into one of San Francisco's wealthiest families, for Lisa McNear Lombardi money was never an issue. Her own mother was an heiress to a cattle fortune — "Tucker" was the surname of her maternal great-great-grandfather — and on the page, the Lombardi family story seemed the stuff of the American Dream. The ambition-driven founding ancestor, Henry Kreiser, came to the U.S. from Germany in 1847 in steerage with five dollars in his pocket, longing to explore the American West. Fate gave him a helping hand when he befriended a man named Henry Miller who, according to a 1998 interview with Kreiser's great-grandson, "had purchased a ticket that took him ostensibly from New York down to the isthmus of Panama, where the parties left the boat and got across the isthmus of Panama any way they could, I think on horses and foot." But on the way, Miller fell in love and decided to stay put, so he sold his ticket the rest of the way to San Francisco to Kreiser. Though he had to assume Miller's identity, Kreiser was able to continue sailing up to California.

He eventually came to own nearly one million acres across three states, which in time grew to three million acres. "It was said that he could ride from Canada to Mexico and be on his own land every day," his great-grandson said.

Along with the land came a bounty of minerals, oil, and gas, and in short order the family was one of the wealthiest in San Francisco, with the fortune bequeathed through a company established by the family, B&N Minerals Partnership.

In 1941, Tucker's maternal grandmother, Mary Ernestine, the heiress to the family fortune, married an insurance broker named Oliver Maurice Lombardi. Lisa was born four years later.

However, Lisa's parents divorced soon after — a relatively rare thing then, even in exalted social circles — and the little girl would not have any semblance of a father figure in her life until her mother remarried in 1963 and took the last name James.

By then Lisa Lombardi was an architecture student at Berkeley, where she met her future husband and Tucker's father, Richard "Dick" Carlson, a reporter for a local San Francisco TV station.

Dick Boynton, later renamed Carlson by his adoptive family, was born in Massachusetts around 1941, out of wedlock to teenage parents — a college student named Richard Boynton, Sr., eighteen, and fifteen-year-old Dorothy Anderson. Dorothy had starved herself to keep the pregnancy secret, resulting in the baby being born with rickets and slightly bent legs. The child was placed in a Boston orphanage called the Home for Little Wanderers, founded after the Civil War to care for children whose fathers failed to return home from battle. Richard Sr., regretting having abandoned his son, soon after concocted a plot to kidnap Dick from the orphanage and elope with Dorothy. But at the last moment, Dorothy refused to go ahead with the plan, and in despair Richard Sr. shot and killed himself two blocks from her home.

Dick Jr. was placed in the care of a foster family, the Mobergers, where he remained for two years, visited by a stream of prospective parents. "I had no real idea why so many folks came to see me, and I just generally thought of them as new friends," Dick wrote in *The Washington Post* in 1993. "My real mother, whose name was Dorothy Anderson, even came, posing as her own sister. She held me, took some photos and disappeared forever. . . . Even Dorothy Anderson's parents, my grandparents, came to visit. I was held briefly by Mrs. Anderson, who cried. Her husband, my grandfather, stood nearby, stern and unspeaking, but looking sad and uncomfortable, according to [Mrs. Moberger]."

In 1943, Dick was adopted by a childless, upper-middle-class New England couple, Ruth and Werner Carlson, of nearby Norwood, Massachusetts. Werner Carlson was an executive at the local Winslow Brothers & Smith Tannery, the oldest tannery in America. Werner had himself grown up fatherless, his dad, a Swedish-born merchant seaman named Axel Carlson, having drowned in Boston harbor when his son was an infant, reportedly after his boat capsized and his feet became tangled in eelgrass.

Werner would pass away when Dick was twelve, and his adoptive mother Ruth fifteen years later, in 1968.

In an era when such things were rarely discussed, for much of his childhood Dick had no idea about the particulars of his background. "I was afraid to ask," he tells me simply.

Not, he adds quickly, that he wants to leave the wrong impression. "Maybe my childhood doesn't sound so great on paper, but it was perfectly okay. People get shortchanged all the time, and whatever shortcomings came with mine, I overcame them."

Dick met Tucker's mother Lisa through her socialite grand-mother, Mrs. Carpenter, who invited the young journalist to the debutante ball where Lisa came out. "I wasn't her escort, but I saw her a lot after that" he recalls evenly. "I thought she was attractive and intelligent and interesting. Also in some ways totally bonkers — but people tend to have a lot of tolerance for that in eccentric girls."

Lisa and Dick were married in 1967 in Carson City, Nevada, and Tucker was born two years later. His only sibling, younger brother Buckley, was born in 1971.

From the start, the Carlson marriage was rocky. A spoiled wild child with no disposition toward motherhood or family, Lisa would become known among acquaintances as an art-world pest reliably drunk or high in social settings — though one with a knack for infil-trating powerful and influential circles. After Dick took a job with KABC-TV in Los Angeles, she reluctantly agreed to move south, and the family lived for a short period in the Laurel Canyon area of Los Angeles — next door, as it happened, to the rock band The Eagles. But when Dick accepted a new job as a local-news anchor in San Diego, Lisa stayed in Los Angeles and he took the boys with him. Dick filed for divorce in 1976, and, maintaining that Lisa's alcohol, marijuana, and cocaine abuse left her incapable of properly caring for Tucker and Buckley, he was granted custody of the boys.

"Lisa made it easier for me, inadvertently," Dick recalls, when, having instigated the custody battle, she failed to show up in court at the arranged date. "Her attorney was embarrassed, he told the judge he didn't know where she was." The judge called the opposing attorneys into his chambers and granted Dick temporary custody — soon to be declared permanent — then and there.

"It was great," says Dick, almost fifty years later, with characteristic understated reserve. "I hadn't been keen to be a father. I never expected it, and I never would have thought of it. But I liked it, and I liked them." He pauses. "I'm eighty—two now, and I hear from them every day, probably because I'm so old." He chuckles. "But they've been a real asset in my life, my emotional life."

Tucker was six years old the last time he saw his mother.

Around the same age, he also first heard the story of his father's birth parents. He vividly recalls the moment. Dick and the boys were in a barber shop, Buckley in the chair getting his haircut, Tucker waiting his turn, as *The Merv Griffin Show* played on the shop's television. The boys were surprised and excited to recognize one of their father's colleagues as a guest on the show. He was on to promote a TV movie the two had worked on together, dealing with the search of adopted adults for their biological parents.

"Well, Merv," he joked to the host, "I'm just a little bastard. The fellow who produced and wrote the show, Dick Carlson, is a little bastard, too."

Hearing the man call their father the dirty word sent the boys flying into a rage. Jumping from the chair, Buckley ripped off his barber cape and shook his fist at the TV.

Carefully, Dick explained the literal meaning of "bastard" — someone whose parents hadn't been married when they were born. And, yes, it was usually a pejorative. But in this case, his friend had appropriated the term, and turned it into a kind of compliment. Reassured, seeming to get it, the boys calmed down.

After their haircuts, the barbershop owner, an elderly Italian man, followed the Carlsons out the door. "Hey, my parents weren't married either, no big deal," he told them.

During an interview in September 2021 on Megyn Kelly's podcast, Kelly questioned Tucker about what happens to a child abandoned by his mother, and if that might lead to trust issues and feeling unlovable.

"I never talked about this because I never want to seem whiney," he replied, "and again, I interpret my childhood as a really positive thing. But our mom was not a fan of us and was pretty direct about it. And, you know, that obviously hurts when you're little. But then I realized you can't control it, you know. You just can't control it, and your mother doesn't like you. Okay, boo hoo, you know. It sounds really terrible, but it's not sort of up to me how she feels. And so, I think in later life the lesson that I internalized from that was you really can't control how other people feel. And, so, you have to just kind of be happy with who you are. I mean I got married at twenty-two and had four kids. So, looking back, it's hard to understand yourself except through your behavior, I think. That's, you know, what you're really like. That's how it manifests itself, and I just had this drive to have a really close, normal, happy family, dinner together, no one's doing anything weird. Do you know what I mean? Also, I grew up in Southern California at a time when people were doing really weird stuff, even by modern standards. And at the time, I knew that when I was little in Laurel Canyon in L.A., I was, like, 'This is weird.' I mean The Eagles lived next door to us. It was like, you know, it's just a wild time in the country. And, so, I didn't want that — I wanted a totally happy family where everyone's close, and everyone's named after someone else, and everyone gets together all the time. And I've had that. And it's the greatest thing in my life, and I really do not take that for granted. And the second thing is criticism from people who hate me doesn't really mean anything to me. I think it really doesn't. I care what the people I love think. I care deeply if my wife is upset with me. I can't even function because I care so much about what she thinks and my children, same thing, my close friends. I have a bunch of lifelong friends. The people I work with, I feel that way about them, too. But like some random, you know, the ADL doesn't like me or something? The partisan who runs it? Like, I don't care. Why would I care? I'm not giving those people emotional control over me. Why? I've been through that. I've lived through that as a child. I'm not doing that again."

"He was a happy little soul," says Dick of his first son, "and always a leader. They had a club — Tucker, Buckley and maybe five of their friends — they'd take off in the morning on their bikes, and be gone till dinner. It never occurred to me it might be dangerous, it wasn't like now. But Tucker always gave the day's marching orders."

Filling out the picture of the idyllic Southern California upscale childhood of yore, Dick produces a photo, *circa* 1968, of Tucker and Buckley on the first day of school. Both wear red-and-pink striped neckties, white shirts, and navy-blue, crested blazers. Tucker has a golden mop of hair and looks sidelong at the camera, flashing a smirk millions of fans would come to recognize.

"I remember I said 'Tucker, you look nice.'" says his father.

"'I look like a midget!'"

Dick laughs. "He was right, he did."

Not long after his divorce, Dick began seeing Patricia Swanson, who lived two houses away and around the corner from the house he and the boys rented in La Jolla. Also born to a legendary American family — her Swedish-immigrant grandfather, Carl A. Swanson, founded the iconic frozen-food company — her family, too, had fallen into dysfunction. According to *The New York Times*, her parents "engaged in long, hysterical battles that the children witnessed," and on her fourteenth birthday, Patricia's mother died from cirrhosis of the liver at forty-eight.

At the time she met Dick Carlson, Patricia was separated from her husband and had an adolescent daughter. Dick says he'd had no intention of remarrying, but "like a lot of women, Patricia liked the idea, and the kids really thought highly of her." So after a couple of years they tied the knot. Patricia ultimately adopted the Carlson boys, their legal names revised as Tucker Swanson McNear Carlson and Buckley Swanson Peck Carlson.

Lisa, meanwhile, having abandoned her children and in open rebellion against the privileged milieu into which she'd been born, continued to fancy herself a free-spirited bohemian. Bumming around the Los Angeles art scene, she got involved with a British-born artist Mo McDermott, who was in the orbit of fellow Brit David Hockney, today one of the most internationally celebrated living artists. Mo became Hockney's assistant, and soon Lisa was attending gallery openings around Los Angeles in his company, as well as soirées at Hockney's Hollywood residence.

Joan Agajanian Quinn, dubbed the matriarch of the Los Angeles art scene and the former West Coast editor of Andy Warhol's *Interview* magazine, recalls Lisa as an art-world groupie who appeared with McDermott at salons Quinn hosted in her Beverly Hills home.

Lisa and Mo McDermott lived in a studio apartment in Hollywood and told people they were married, but no documentation of the marriage seems to exist. They jointly produced sculptures and exhibited around galleries in Los Angeles. The duo were known for heavy indulgence in drugs and alcohol and engaging in explosive arguments.

"I remember she was taller than Mo," Quinn recalls. "She had chopped, spiky hair. She was unkempt. She never looked clean to me.

"Mo was very charming and impish. Lisa was more direct. But as time went on, she became more antagonistic, fighting with him a lot. When I saw them at David Hockney's studio or at an art opening, they would usually be arguing. I didn't realize at the time she was probably under the influence. I thought she was trying really hard to be arty, but I didn't think she was an artist. She was kind of hippy dippy. I thought she was cashing in on Mo's connection to Hockney."

Although details remain vague, they appear to have been together until McDermott's death from liver failure in 1988.

Quinn owns three or four colorful wood sculptures produced by the pair. They're of trees: palm and eucalyptus. "They're very loose and have this quality of life to them. They have a movement," she says of the sculptures. "I still have them, I love them. They're happy. So, Lisa and Mo must have been happy together at one time, even though I remember them just arguing all the time."

Art collector Molly Barnes exhibited Lisa and Mo's work in the early 1980s and told *Business Insider* that Lisa "had come from a lot of money and that reflected on her personality. She wasn't a snob in any way but she had the manners of a private school girl. Someone who was fighting the establishment."

In a photograph taken at the time of that exhibition, one of the few known to publicly exist, Lisa towers over Mo McDermott, who is significantly shorter. At first glance Lisa doesn't look recognizably female. She wears straight-legged jeans cuffed at the ankles, work boots, and a collared shirt with both hands tucked into the pockets of a blazer. Her feathered, tousled hair is a man's cut. She's not wearing makeup. She has a wide stance and masculine posture and she bites her lower lip in a pugnacious smirk.

McDermott, for his part, was long rumored to be gay or bisexual. The year after his death, Lisa married British painter Michael Vaughan, another peer of David Hockney and a fellow member of the so-called Bradford Mafia collective of artists. They split their time between Cazac, in the south of France, and the Sea Islands of South Carolina, until Lisa's death from cancer on October 14, 2011.

During her life, Lisa failed to attract recognition as a solo artist and continued to piggyback on her more famous husbands. Eight months before her death, Lisa and Michael Vaughan exhibited a series of jointly created artworks at London's prestigious Redfern Gallery, where one critic called the works "cheerful but disturbing art."

An obituary published in the *San Francisco Chronicle* described Tucker's mother, now Lisa Lombardi-Vaughan, as a fifth-generation Californian survived by three siblings. Her prior marriage to Dick, and her two sons, Tucker and Buckley, were omitted.

In October 2011, Tucker received a phone call from a relative who told him his estranged mother, now living in France, was dying. He was forty-two years old and working as a contributor at Fox News.

He told Megyn Kelly: "I've always said to my wife, the whole time, I was like, she never met my mother, obviously, and I said, I feel great about it. I feel totally fine. I feel very well-adjusted, especially when I stopped partying. But I'm kind of worried I'm going to get a call one day from someone, like this woman's been found dead, and we think that she's your mother or whatever. I don't know anything about her. I don't know where she is. I'm totally cut off. I mean I — and I said to my wife for years, I would say I hope it doesn't trigger some collapse or something, or I go crazy. And the day it actually happened, I got this call, she's dying, and in this weird little town and set on a farm that she lived on in southwestern France and she was basically French at this point, spent her life there — uh, you should go visit her. And, so, I called my brother, and he's like, 'What? No. You know my son's got a soccer game.' And I said, I feel the same way. I don't know this person. And actually this sounds cold or whatever, but I had already kind of made my peace with this over many decades, over thirty-five years. And I didn't fall apart at all. I went out to dinner. I mean I felt sad for her, I guess. I don't know much about her. She was an artist. She had shows, okay, I guess, and all that, but she wasn't part of my life. I wasn't part of hers. And I just — I don't know."

But it's hard not to suspect it's not quite so simple. "My father's most acid insult ever delivered was about my biological mother," he tells me one evening, largely out of context, since we've been talking about literature, "I'll never forget it. She was quite smart, but not serious as a person, and obviously really flawed in a lot of other ways. I asked him one day, was she smart? And he said, 'Well, yes, but she read magazines.'" Tucker laughed that distinctive laugh. "Like, she couldn't do the work to continue the thread for three hundred pages."

Although he never saw her again after the age of six, according to his wife, Susie, Tucker did have contact with his mother two or three times. "It had to have had an effect on him, how could it not?" she tells me. "We can only control our own responses to trauma, or rejection, or whatever the issues are in our lives. At a very young age, he recognized that. But I think he didn't focus on it. He chose to think about his dad and his brother and those relationships and to feel grateful for that. He said to me, 'I'm lucky I didn't have to grow up under the same roof as a crazy person. A lot of people have one parent who's crazy and they're way more affected, right? Because they're living day to day with this person.' He didn't have to and he's grateful for that."

Later, in another context, Tucker would tell me his thoughts on Freudian psychiatry, which was once almost universally respected, but in recent decades has been roundly "dismissed as total crackpot, self-absorbed bullshit. And I agree that in its details a lot of it *was* completely silly. But Freudian psychology was a huge force. That way of thinking was universal in the United States — people would ascribe motives to human behavior that were based in your childhood, your lived experience. People would do things, and the explanation that you'd hear would be like, well, you know, he had some conflict with his mother in his childhood, or severe toilet training. People talked like that. And a lot of it was silly, Freud himself was kind of silly, but that way of thinking was real. There's a lot going on inside of people that has to do with the experiences they've had. You are a product to some extent of genetics but also, to another hard-to-quantify extent, the product of the life you have lived and the emotions that life has generated within you. Now, we've just reduced people to chemicals. Someone decided chemistry could describe human behavior. I don't know who decided that — probably the biotech firms, pharma. But what it's done, in effect, is gotten everyone on drugs, which is the trend in American life I hate most. Secondarily, or maybe even more importantly, it ended the conversation about why people do the things they do and why they feel the way they do. Why do you feel that way? There are clearly biochemical reasons for depression, I'm not pretending that's not true, but for the overwhelming majority of people anxiety and depression are signs that you're not living in the right way. If you burn your finger on the stove and someone says to you, 'I have a painkiller that will make that go away so the next time you touch the stove you won't feel anything,' you'd say, *wait a second!* Maybe your body is telling you that your flesh is burning off and you shouldn't touch the stove. Maybe it's a sign that you should change your behavior. And that used to be much more obvious. Like Freud, as silly as he was in some ways, pointed us back to something real, which was: the way you live matters.

When Tucker was twenty-one and preparing to ask for Susie's hand in marriage, he did get Lisa's address from her sister. Recalls Susie: "He wrote her a letter and said, 'I'm writing to tell you, my mother, that I am asking a woman to marry me, and I'm writing to tell you I forgive you for what you did to me as a child, because I know I will never be the kind of husband and father I hope to be if I cannot forgive you.' So, he was never bitter. He truly forgave her."

Susie says that Lisa called once after the couple were married. She answered the phone. "I'd never heard her voice before. She was drunk and wanted to talk to Tucker. I told him, 'It's Lisa,' and he took the phone. I don't know what she said on her end, but he said to her, 'I'm not going to talk to you if you've been drinking. If you want to have a conversation with me, please call me when you're not drunk.' And he hung up," Susie recalls.

Susie remembers well the day Lisa died. They were at their home in D.C. Tucker's stepmother was planning a Christmas party to benefit a local Christian ministry, and she'd gotten a lot of presents for the ministry's nuns and residents and packed up a U-Haul to store them at Tucker and Susie's. As Dick, Buckley, and Tucker moved boxes from the U-Haul to the garage, crossing paths to and from the truck, Dick nonchalantly said, "Oh, yeah, Lisa died."

Susie was some distance away, and unsure what she'd heard, she asked the brothers: "Did he just tell you that your mother died?" It was as though Dick had commented on the weather. "That's so Pop," one of them said, smiling. Neither cried.

Not that even then Lisa was completely out of their lives. In 1995, a lawyer had estimated the value of Lisa's estate at $2.6 million, though that appears to have been vastly depleted by the time she died. In 2013, a court ruled that Lisa died intestate and her wealth would be divided into three equal portions: one to her husband Michael Vaughan, one to her son Buckley, and one to her son Tucker. Vaughan signed paperwork that confirmed and agreed with this decision.

Soon after, one of Vaughan's daughters from a previous marriage claimed to have discovered a handwritten, one-page will tucked into the pages of a book that Lisa left behind. Michael Vaughan claimed he'd forgotten about the existence of this will when he agreed to the three-way split of assets. The newly found document purportedly left all of Lisa's estate to Vaughan — save two dollars. A codicil to the one-page will stated, "I leave my sons Tucker Swanson McNear Carlson and Buckley Swanson Peck Carlson one dollar each."

Aside from being a fuck-you to the children she'd abandoned, a one-dollar inheritance often is used to thwart disputes over an estate. According to court documents, Lisa's estate, a 1/32 share in interest and royalties from the family's landholdings, totaled less than $150,000. Still, a protracted legal battle ensued. A hand-writing expert testified the will did come from Lisa. One of Lisa's siblings became involved and took the side of the Carlsons. "Michael Vaughan can sell his share and leave the rest of us alone," she said in a court hearing. Eventually in 2019, the California Appellate Court ruled with the Carlsons, allowing the brothers to keep shares of their estranged mother's estate.

From the start Dick had been the constant, steady presence in his boys' lives. As soon as they could walk, he dragged them along to dinners, restaurants, work events, and reporting gigs to ensure, as he says, that they "became well-informed and early gourmands." Regular dinner guests in the Carlson home included Republican San Diego mayor and future California governor Peter Wilson, as well as Theodore Geisel, the children's book author internationally renowned as Dr. Seuss.

He also exposed them to his highly distinctive line of work. One afternoon out reporting with his young sons in tow, Dick led the boys beyond the yellow crime-scene tape to get a closer inspection of a murder victim splayed on the sidewalk. On another assignment, he took them along for an up-close look at a raging wildfire in Santa Barbara, where they slept on the smoldering ground beside a fire engine. Once when they were five and six, they went along for a Sunday dinner at the San Fernando Valley home of Eddie Canniz-zaro, a notorious mobster and the prime suspect in a 1947 Beverly

Hills mafia hit. Cannizzaro and his father, Joe, an ex-gunman and driver for Al Capone, gave the Carlson boys a tour of the garden and showed them how to make pasta e fagioli. According to Dick, when the father and son got into a heated argument, Joe backhanded Eddie so hard his nose bled. "My boys were even more impressed," recalls Dick in his unpublished memoir. "'See what happens when you cross your father,' said Joe to the boys, patting them on the head. Eddie's mother just smiled from the other end of the table and offered Tucker and Buckley more homemade cannoli-cream cake."

From the outset, what might be called Dick's lessons in manhood by example shaped the boys in vital ways.

One of Tucker's formative childhood memories involves an episode that in today's world would have had Child Protective Services beating down the family door. It occurred on a dirt road in California when he was seven. Dick was teaching the boys how to "car surf." "We are lying face down on the roof of our family's 1976 Ford Country Squire station wagon, a wood-paneled land yacht almost nineteen feet long," Tucker would fondly recall in a 2015 essay. "My father is in the driver's seat smoking a Pall Mall. 'Hold on,' he yells through the open window. My brother and I grip the leading edge of the luggage rack, spaying our legs like snipers. My father guns the massive V8 and we shoot forward at high speed over culvert and potholes and rocks. At one especially steep hump in the road we seem to catch air and I look over in time to see my brother in flight, tethered to the vehicle only by his fingertips."

Tucker wondered exactly what this was meant to teach. "Was he trying to instill in us a proper sense of fatalism, the acknowledgement that there is only so much in life you can control? Or was it a lesson about the importance of risk? Until you're willing to ride the roof of a speeding station wagon, in other words, you're probably not going to leave your mark on the world."

Dick was always at war with the uptight moms in the neighborhood. Early on, he gave his sons M-80s and lawn darts for toys, and both boys were driving by thirteen. Tucker learned on a rented, stick-shift station wagon with just an AM radio, on which he'd pick up outlaw radio stations from Tijuana. He and Buckley would drive around town listening to loud Mexican pop music. At fifteen, when his father told him he needed to go to driver's ed to get a license, Tucker drove himself there each day for the weeklong course.

"I remember the third day of the class I'm sitting next to this stoner with the blonde butt-cut, the Puka shell necklace, and I show up late, and he looks up at me and goes, 'Wait. This is a driver's ed course. We're here to get our licenses. But you drove. How did you do that?'" Tucker laughs, doing his best Jeff Spicoli impersonation. "Because my dad lets me do anything!"

Another life lesson Dick imparted by repeated example had to do with perspective. For instance, Tucker still recalls the morning a couple in a San Diego Denny's restaurant approached local news anchor Dick and asked if he'd sign the menu. After complying, Dick watched the couple walk off and turned to his young sons. "Those people mean well," he told them, "but two years from now they're not even going to remember my name."

Dick knows from personal experience how often "people in television, who get paid huge amounts of money, think they're important," as he tells me. "But Tucker's not like that — not overly impressed with himself, or thinking he's got all the answers. He has humility." He pauses, recalls running into a man for whom Tucker worked when he was starting out in his journalism career. "'I just want to tell you why I hired your son,' he said. "It's because he had such good manners. We had over a hundred people apply for the job and I interviewed them. Your son didn't have any experience in newspapers, but his manners were so outrageously good that it affected me, and I hired him for that reason. He stood up when I entered the room, he looked me in the eye when he shook my hands." Dick pauses. "Then he went on from there to *The Weekly Standard*, and next thing I knew he's flying off to war zones. He was a good boy. More parents should be as lucky as I was."

"[My father] once said to me, life is difficult at times but it's not that hard to be happy if you put your mind to it," Tucker told an audience in Des Moines, Iowa, in 2022. "And my father's happiness comes from his family — we have the world's closest family, I would say — and dogs, and his wife, and nature, and reading, and that's been enough. So, in every sense he's a model for me. Not just because he's the toughest man I've ever met in my life. He was the only dad in the rich little town I grew up in who would punch people out over a parking space, and he wouldn't even hesitate. It's such a different world now.

"I remember this girl in my second-grade class was, like, 'Tucker's dad's crazy,' and I was, like, my dad is not crazy! You know, maybe a little crazy. But tough in the sense [that] he would never complain, period, under any circumstances. As one of my kids said, if grandfather was on fire, he'd be, like, 'Totally fine. It's fine.' And I just feel like that's because he doesn't want to burden other people. And that self-pity is root of all suffering."

Indeed, this is the way the family much later discovered Dick had prostate cancer. During dinner one night, he casually remarked that he needed a ride to the hospital the next day.

Over the years, first father and now son have devoted great effort to ensure a reset on the family lineage of dysfunction and abandonment. It is not for nothing that Tucker regularly punches at a shibboleth of the free-market, pro-business right, which often relegates family to a second-tier consideration. This is something few Republicans dare confront, and certainly no other cable news host, their livelihoods dependent on corporatism. But for Tucker, family is key to everything.

"The unchanging fact is, your work actually doesn't mean very much, in the end," as he told his audience in Des Moines. "Imagine a ruling class, the people with actual power, committed to telling young people that it does. And doing so with the aide and financial backing of the biggest companies in the country. They're promoting the idea your family is worthless compared to loyalty to your employer and a political party. That is the sickest message I can possibly imagine. It's a totalitarian message."

Over dinner one night, Tucker lets drop that by fourteen, he was an inveterate hitchhiker.

"Hitchhiking?" I say in surprise. Though just a generation younger, I grew up hearing the custom was akin to offering oneself up as prey for every passing serial killer and deranged long distance trucker.

His expression becomes gravely perplexed, as though I've challenged something obvious and fundamental, like the existence of God. "Of course," he says, definitively, "hitchhiking."

He tells of how in the summer before tenth grade he was enrolled in the Outward Bound program in Maine, living in the wilderness for a month, and at the end of the program, all the other parents came to pick up their children. But Dick sent a note to say he wasn't coming. "I'll be at the house," it read. "I'll see you there. I know you can make your way back."

"He wrote me every day," says Tucker. "He was such a wonderful, committed father. But he was not the kind of guy who picked you up, because why would he prevent you from having a life-changing experience with hitchhiking?"

Tucker hadn't showered in a month. But, duffel bag in hand, he hit the road with his scraggly, adolescent beard and stuck his thumb out. Two girls immediately picked him up and took him to the movies, and he was on his way. He made it home, no problem.

In college, he and his roommate hitched from Maine to Nova Scotia, where Carlson's family had some land, a small island. So, the pair thought, 'Fuck it, let's check it out.' They brought camping gear and ended up lost and marooned in a national forest.

"My father was definitely encouraging that, all the time, push your limits," Carlson says.

Once Dick and the boys relocated to San Diego in 1974, and Dick took on the responsibilities of lead anchor on local CBS affiliate KFMB-TV, he hired help to assist around the Carlson's La Jolla home, and family lore features an array of loopy housekeepers who played a role in the Carlson ménage. There was the terse, widowed German woman who served boiled potatoes and cabbage for every meal; the twenty-five-year-old man who stole jewelry and expressed too much interest in the neighborhood's underage girls; the unmarried Mormon nurse who, if Dick was out late, perched waiting at the kitchen table when he got home, agitated in her bathrobe, interrogating him about his whereabouts; and the Alabama debutante who drained the liquor cabinet and left the family dog nearly to starve.

A string of Asian housemen became another staple in the Carlson home. First there was a Japanese man who lived with the family in Los Angeles. He was replaced by a Korean named Mr. Yang, whose father had been the chief of police in Seoul; when the North Koreans swept over the border in 1950 the family went underground. "My childhood was filled with stories of the Korean War because we had Mr. Yang living with us and he would tell us what it was like hiding from the communists as a kid," Tucker remembers over dinner one night. "He was a really big part of my life." When Mr. Yang eventually got married, the wedding was held on the Carlsons' front lawn, and he and his wife moved to another part of California to open a liquor store in a blighted neighborhood. "He was an amazingly tough person. They were afraid of him in the 'hood. He'd take his shirt off and beat you with a belt if you tried to rob him," Carlson says. They've kept in contact ever since. "I heard from him two weeks ago."

Mr. Yang left and was replaced by Colonel Kwon, a retired Korean army colonel and "a wonderful man who had a huge effect on me." Colonel Kwon, his wife, and three children lived with the Carlsons for several years. "It was a full immersion into Korean culture. My whole life we had Koreans living with us. Colonel Kwon was the only uninjured and surviving member of his military class in Seoul. So he had a really tough time during the war. But he survived," Carlson says.

"He grew up speaking Japanese, under the Japanese occupation of Korea. We grew up hearing a lot of anti-Japanese propaganda.

He and Mr. Yang both read Japanese and watched Japanese movies because they'd grown up under occupation. Korean was illegal. For forty years, until 1945, the Japanese were true cultural imperialists: no Korean names, no Korean language, no Korean culture, period. So they both hated Japan. But then they'd take us to Japanese restaurants. It was so weird."

Carlson laughs about his childhood. "Not average! It sounds so weird. I've never thought about it until right now. But it was honestly great. My father is a full egalitarian. If he likes you, you're eating at the dinner table with us. So Mr. Yang and Colonel Kwon were full members of the family. It's not like they were servants scurrying around."

One Thanksgiving when Tucker was in the tenth grade, Colonel Kwon's wife cooked dinner. "She was a wonderful cook. For Thanksgiving, my parents always invited all the randoms — alcoholics, widows — it was always a full performance at the table."

Dick leaned over to Colonel Kwon and asked: After the war, when they were pushing North Korean forces back over the thirty-eighth parallel, how did you know who was from the North and who was from the South?

"The hair. You feel the heads. North Koreans have shaved heads. You feel bald head, you stab them in the neck with bayonet," Colonel Kwon said. "He was transfixed," Tucker recalls. "There are all these women around the table, our neighbors, these super liberals. And he goes, 'And we take prisoners. We used them for bayonet practice. *Go-go-go-go!*" he imitates, making a rapid jabbing motion. "'And then we took them, and tie dynamite to heads. And daisy chain them. And *Boom!* Blow off head.' I remember everyone's faces at the table. The women were dying. But how do you tell Colonel Kwon to stop? I was

67

loving it. To me, that moment is indelible. Watching my father, who is very catlike and doesn't portray emotion, his eye was twitching. I could tell he was like, *I've got to get Colonel Kwon to shut up. My wife's going to get super mad at me,*" Tucker laughs.

"I was really greatly enriched by that," he says. "I went to Colonel Kwon's funeral, maybe three years ago. I was sobbing with his three children. It was really moving. All funerals are moving, all rituals are moving, of course. But that was my childhood. You'll see, when you have people die who were important to you as a kid. It's about them, but it's also about you. It's the end of something. That whole world is gone. I can't even imagine living like that anymore. But that's OK; it's replaced by new things. But it all just comes to you."

CHAPTER
FOUR

His childhood immersion in magazines certainly played a part, and the eye-popping work of Hunter Thompson, but more than anything else, it was the most old-fashioned of impulses that set Tucker on the path to become a journalist: it's what his father did.

To this day they speak daily, and Tucker unhesitatingly describes Dick as his greatest mentor. "I always had the feeling that there was something not-quite-mainstream about what he did for a living. It was like he belonged to a secret organization with a slightly different set of rules," writes Tucker in the introduction to his father's unpublished memoir. "He never came out and declared journalists were exempt from the usual bourgeois regulations, but that was definitely the sense. Watching him, I got the impression that reporters weren't part of the straight world. As far as my father was concerned, interesting experiences weren't a perk of journalism, they were the point of it. Journalism was the chance to experience the world, to see things other people didn't. Journalism was adventure."

Dick had been bored in high school. "I wanted to be a writer or literary bon vivant or a warrior or anything other than what I was destined to be by circumstance and geography," he wrote. On summer break from Ole Miss, he took a job as a police officer in the resort community of Ocean City, Maryland, believing the experience would prime him with characters and stories for his future career as a writer. In 1963, he got a break when a chance encounter landed him a job as a copyboy at the *Los Angeles Times*. He moved on from there to become a staff writer at United Press International; then, in 1966, to KGO-TV in San Francisco, covering street crime and municipal corruption.

It was *interesting* work. One night, staking out a murderer in a sketchy neighborhood, he was shocked to see some guy pull out a gun directly in front of him and shoot down a pair of hippies. When the killer confessed his motive — *he was sick of longhaired freaks screwing up his town!* — Dick was grateful he'd gone to work in loafers and slacks that night, rather than in a caftan.

The murderer Dick was casing that night? His victim was a drug dealer, who would be caught after he brought the victim's arm to his mother's house to be boiled on her kitchen stove.

Later, as political editor of Los Angeles's KABC-TV, Dick formed the station's investigative-reporting unit. His 1972 documentary, *Pounds of Sadness*, on the abuse and neglect at Los Angeles dog shelters, would win an Emmy. Like his subsequent work about children of adoption, the story was highly personal for Dick; forty years after two of his own dogs died, he still carries their pictures in his wallet.

Still at KABC, Dick earned national recognition, as well as a Peabody Award, for a thirty-four-part series exposing extensive fraud involving the supposedly revolutionary three-wheeled auto The Dale, advertised as getting seventy-miles-per-gallon during the 1970s energy crisis. Among other things, Dick exposed the fact that the president and public face of the company, G. Elizabeth Carmichael, who'd received rapturous media attention as a groundbreaking female CEO (a sort of Elizabeth Holmes avant la lettre) was in actuality not only a biological man, born Jerry Dean Michael, who'd fathered ten children with four different women, but a career criminal on the lam facing federal charges for counterfeiting. Dick Carlson's reporting resulted in thirty-nine indictments against Carmichael and other executives of the Twentieth Century Motor Company, named after the fictional business in Ayn Rand's *Atlas Shrugged*.

Perhaps inevitably, the story would resurface in our own confused age. In a 2021 HBO documentary called *The Lady and the Dale*, the career fraudster Carmichael is sympathetically recast as a transgender trailblazer, while the dogged journalist Dick, who is interviewed extensively, is linked to his son Tucker as part of a dark, generational transphobia passed from father to son. Indeed, the documentary makes much of the fact that it was Dick Carlson who had also reported that women's professional tennis player Renee Richards had formerly been Richard Raskind, touching off the Seventies' greatest trans-related media sensation.

As *Out* magazine headlined its story on *The Lady and the Dale*, "This Docuseries Could Explain Why Tucker Carlson Hates Trans Women."

Dick Carlson bristles at the suggestion that his enterprising reporting, at the time recognized as courageous, demands any apology. "It was a great story, that's how I looked at it, period. I had no hostility to Richards, and over the years we talked a few times. It was a smear job."

Nonetheless, to no one's surprise, the 2022 GLAAD (Gay & Lesbian Alliance Against Defamation) Media Awards named *The Lady and the Dale* the year's Outstanding Documentary.

In 1984, by now a highly visible media figure in San Diego, Dick ran for mayor as a Republican. In a contentious race against the incumbent, he lost. But the following year, Ronald Reagan named him associate director of the U.S. Information Agency and the family moved to Washington, D.C. Under Reagan, Dick would run the Voice of America, with a daily global audience of 130 million, as well as Radio Martí, its counterpart broadcasting into Cuba.

Since Voice of America had in the past been closely aligned with the CIA, and Dick acknowledges he had friends in the Agency, which inevitably "rubs off on you a bit," it has been speculated that Tucker Carlson's father was himself an agent, but Dick scoffs at the notion.

What is true is that while in college, Tucker himself applied to join the CIA and was turned down, he tells me, because he couldn't pass the drug test. "Can you imagine me, someone who can't follow direction and hates authority in the CIA?" he later laughingly asks me.

In 1991, Dick left Voice of America, when George H.W. Bush named him ambassador to the Seychelles, the archipelago nation off the coast of Africa. When, the following year, he was appointed CEO of the Corporation for Public Broadcasting, Dick found himself in the awkward position of defending an enterprise the Republican Party had turned decisively against. At a 1993 fundraiser for the Boston orphanage where he'd spent time as a child, Dick remarked on the irony that despite his own considerable and well earned misgivings about broadcast media, "in spite of its faults and occasional moronic biases and the fact that television itself has contributed indisputably to the dumbing down of America, the amazing stupidization of an entire country," he continued to stubbornly believe public broadcasting was a net good for society.

CHAPTER
FIVE

Tucker makes no secret of the fact, like his father, he had little interest in school. As a student he had crippling dyslexia, problems with spatial relations and hand-eye coordination, and complex math problems were out of the question.

"I was a total loser, academically," as he told Janice Dean on her podcast in the fall of 2022. "I had an almost uninterrupted string of Ds from about third grade until I finally got married at the end of college."

But also like Dick, he was an avid reader — finishing *War and Peace* before he was ten.

"I got my education through reading," he tells me one evening, relaxing in a Boca Grande, Florida, restaurant called The Temptation, after doing his show from its winter quarters. As usual, he sits with his back to the room to avoid attracting attention.

"There was just a huge emphasis at home on reading," he continues. "Although my father had this weird bigotry against American literature — except for Steinbeck, and John O'Hara, they were OK. And I also loved Steinbeck. I've read almost everything, even his weird, obscure shit, like his post-war Soviet propaganda. But other than that, we did not read American literature at all. My father was very anti-Faulkner and anti-Hemingway, the stuff that everyone lionizes. On the other hand, the Brits, Evelyn Waugh or Arthur Conan Doyle, it's insane they're so good! That was his view and that was definitely also my view."

Tucker loves that the restaurant is a truly old-fashioned joint, its walls vintage murals of palm trees, lighthouses, beachgoers, and fishing boats, the neon sign out front, a tilted martini glass. He pauses now, as a young restaurant staffer approaches.

"Thank you for serving us dinner at this late hour," he tells her, "I'm pretty excited."

"Oh, I just pour the water," she replies, blushing.

"No, you do more than that. That's a critical link in the chain. You're greeting us at the restaurant and setting the tone for the entire meal."

"I was a dishwasher," he tells me as she moves off, "and I felt like a critical part of the restaurant. I was the one who pulled the cigarette butts out of the hollandaise sauce — and there were a lot of those, and you couldn't run them through the dishwasher. People would sit there and grind their smokes out into their eggs benedict." He laughs. "Eggs B with Marlboro Lights."

He pauses a moment, before picking up the earlier thread. "Also I loved Russian literature. Unbelievable — Dostoevsky and of course

Tolstoy. I just read the *Kreutzer Sonata*, which is one of his shorter novels. It's brilliant. Tolstoy got really dark and really crazy in his old age, ultimately ran away from his wife and died on a train. And the *Kreutzer Sonata* is about how evil sex is. Tolstoy was a crazed womanizer — he was just out banging serfs, like they all did, a woman was your property. And then he gets married in his thirties and remains married to the same woman until he's in his eighties, and really torments her toward the end. He stopped sleeping with her when she was in her fifties — he was, like, that's disgusting I'm not doing that anymore. He started to really hate sex, and became an anti-sex activist, which is about as far from my view as you can get." He pauses. "But there's this wholesale dismissal of Russian culture by people who've never read a book, telling you Russia is just a gas station with an army. It's, like, fuck you, you philistine, you don't know anything. Don't lecture me on other cultures, moron!"

He takes a sip of water. "Of course, some of it is pretty tough going, I just read a bunch of Gogol short stories this year, and by the end I was like, 'Whoa! I'm too shallow for this! Maybe something slightly less brooding next time.'"

What he learned from his dad, he concludes, was "to be intentional about what you read. Find good books and read them. Don't just pick up whatever's sitting there."

What's more than a little odd about this conversation — or monologue, really — is that there is a subject far distant from Tolstoy and Gogol that, for almost anyone else in his field, would at this moment be of overriding and likely extreme concern. For it was just a few minutes earlier that he learned what Paul Ryan — former House Speaker and, more to the point, a member of the Fox board — said on a podcast earlier in the day. Asked by a liberal questioner why he didn't push back against the "toxic sludge, racism, disinformation, and attacks on democracy" at the network, Ryan replied that the "screed you just made on Fox, I think that was probably just Tucker," adding that he and Carlson are "different kinds of conservatives."

When I raise Ryan's remark, Tucker just flashes a grin. "When a board member from your company attacks you, probably not a good sign!"

He considers for an instant. "Something I've always noticed is how transitory these things we take to be important are, and how fast things change." He pauses half a beat, then shouts: "Moose!"

"Moose?"

He smiles, launches into the story. "One morning in Maine I'm doing seventy, on my way to go fishing. Middle of nowhere, five thirty in the morning. I'd always bring my dog fishing, every morning, and she'd sit in the front seat with me, always. This dog is keen on fishing, she's spent a lifetime doing it. She knows the whole protocol for fly-fishing, how the dog has to stand behind you so she doesn't spook the pool. It was early June, our trout season ends in mid-June, and I woke up this morning so excited to go fishing. I was leaving for Japan in three days, and I really wanted to get this in. And I didn't take the dog. My wife asked why, and I said I didn't know. I just wasn't taking the dog. Well, I hit this moose going seventy — I was coming over this rise in outlaw country, just grooving out and all of a sudden there's this giant nose in the windshield. Totaled my truck. A moose is so big you can't even believe it's real. And the dog would have been killed by the airbag, for sure."

The waitress arrives and Carlson orders the fried shrimp.

"Would you like a vegetable?" she asks.

"Absolutely not," he says, with certainty.

"My wife eats that poison," he confides, after she's retreated with our order, "but I don't eat vegetables at all, period, under any circumstances. That's the commitment I made to myself forty years ago, 1983, when I was at boarding school, and I've really stuck with it. I'm fourteen, I'm going off to boarding school and what changes am I going to make now that I can do whatever I want? One, I'm going to use as much tobacco as I can, and two, I'm never going to have another vegetable ever again. Iceberg lettuce is the exception," he notes, almost parenthetically, "but I don't think that's a vegetable, it's just paper and water — a platform for blue cheese and bacon and that's how I use it."

Which brings us back to the topic with which we began, his troubles with school.

In first grade, at La Jolla's exclusive Country Day School, overlooking the Pacific, Tucker was put in a class for students with learning disabilities. "The proctor would show up and take the dumb kids out, and I was in the dumb kids, the cohort that got pulled out of class, and I really resented it because I didn't think I was dumb," he told Janice Dean. "I grew up with a dad who was wise enough to not say, 'Oh, you've got learning disabilities.' He just didn't mention it. I love to read, so reading really saved me. I've always liked words; they were my refuge. They make sense to me. I've always been fluent and I think that's compensation for my deficiencies."

CHAPTER
SIX

In 1983, Tucker left home for St. George's School, a private, co-ed, Episcopalian boarding school in Middleton, Rhode Island, just east of Newport.

Designed by landscape architect Frederick Law Olmsted, co-architect of New York's Central Park, the campus, dominated by a stone neo-Gothic church, is perched atop a cliff overlooking the Atlantic. The student body, grades nine through twelve, numbered fewer than four hundred, and even now boys are required to wear coat and tie. Tuition and boarding today runs around $69,650 a year. Notable, festooned alumni include members of the Gilded Age Astor family, former Rhode Island governor William Henry Vanderbilt III, former Vermont governor Howard Dean, George H.W. Bush's father Prescott Bush, and Bush family cousin TV host Billy Bush, of *Access Hollywood* fame. The next most famous member of the class of 1987, aside from Tucker, is actress Julie Bowen, known for her role as Claire

Dunphy on the ABC sitcom *Modern Family*. (Bowen did not respond to requests to be interviewed for this book).

"I think we had a reputation for well-to-do but not necessarily bright kids, at least not as bright as that, or they would have gone to Andover or St. Paul's," Rusty Rushton, Tucker's former English teacher at St. George's and today a professor at the University of Alabama, Birmingham, tells me. "It was still a good place, a good school with good faculty."

Keller Kimbrough, a classmate at St. George's and now the chair of the department of Asian languages and civilizations at the University of Colorado-Boulder, remembers Tucker as a charming rabble-rouser.

"He was always very articulate and smart, and a real bullshitter. He didn't seem to me particularly ideological, he just loved to be provocative. We would talk about current events and all kinds of stuff, politics, and he'd be happy to argue any side of an argument, he didn't really care. He was just as happy to argue a liberal point of view as a conservative point of view. He just enjoyed the argument and liked winning whatever side he was on, especially when he could do it with flair."

Kimbrough remembers one night, when a group were drinking in his dorm room, that the conversation turned to religion, and "Tucker pulls out his wallet and removes a card saying he's an ordained minister. He'd written away to some catalog where for eight or ten dollars they send you an ordination card, and he'd saved it for just this kind of occasion. So he pulls out the card and says, 'Well, you should know I'm telling you this from the perspective of an ordained minister . . .' I was, like, 'Wow, *that* was a good move!'"

Drinking was of course a favorite pastime for the boys at St. George's, and Tucker and Kimbrough spent countless hours getting drunk in Kimbrough's dorm room. "We would sneak in booze and get into these kind of informal debates. He just loved to talk about stuff, and he was really good at it."

Their larger social world centered around the sixth-form smoking porch, a colonnaded wooden porch overlooking the Atlantic where students were allowed to smoke cigarettes until the administration cracked down and moved the smoking area to an alleyway next to a dumpster.

It was at St. George's that Tucker met his future wife. Susie Andrews was the daughter of the school's newly installed headmaster, Reverend George Andrews, the school's previous headmaster having abruptly departed after reports that some students, both male and female, had been sexually abused by employees dating back to the 1970s.

The first day of Tucker's tenth-grade year, Susie, pretty and blonde, walked into class, having just enrolled at St. George's as a sophomore. Tucker was smitten at first sight. At the time he was dating another girl at the school, but, he recalled on a podcast interview, "I was, like, 'Oh, wow!' I was totally blown away. And I don't know if she's the prettiest girl at school, I have no idea, but to me she was. Her father was the headmaster of the school and that's scary. I was bold. She was too cute. I couldn't help it. One thing I'll say about love and lust, it does make you brave."

Two weeks into the school year, Susie tells me, in the native Upper Midwest accent about which Tucker still teases her, she was in the basement after study hall buying some chips and soda and talking with friends when she saw Tucker across the room. "I said to my friend, 'like, who is that?' Because I thought he was so cute. And my friend said, 'That's Tucker Carlson, you want to stay away from him. Anyway, he has a girlfriend.'"

But soon after, Susie was sitting on the quad with another friend and Tucker came walking up with his L.L. Bean bag, khaki pants, and a *New York Times* under his arm and introduced himself. "I was totally gaga. I'm a fifteen-year-old girl. So the three of us started talking. Reagan was running for president at the time, and I couldn't believe how much he knew about politics. And then our friend left, and we continued talking. It got to be about five thirty and he asked if I wanted to go get pizza. So we walked down the hill to this pizza restaurant and we had dinner, and that was it."

Tucker broke up with his girlfriend the next day.

Once Tucker started dating Susie, who did not drink or smoke, his friends saw a lot less of him. "In his junior year, he just stopped hanging out with the people who did that," Kimbrough says. "Susie had a very positive influence on him."

While Kimbrough, who identifies as a Democrat, these days keeps his long-ago association with Carlson largely under wraps — "Frankly, it would be damaging to me to make that widely known" — he tells me Tucker "was a good guy, and I have no hard feelings whatsoever."

That said, based on the kid he knew at St. George's, he has theories about the Tucker Carlson the world sees today, chalking up "some asinine things" he says "to his desire to be provocative and somewhat shocking. Because I know his personality, and it's just the way he is."

Tucker's onetime English teacher, Rushton, also a Democrat, is considerably less generous. Recalling Tucker and Susie in school, he says he didn't understand what she saw in him — and is very surprised to learn they are still happily married with four children. Susie was "quite wonderful," he says. "What she emanated was sweet, not ditsy, perfectly intelligent, upbeat, kind, warm. She probably got the best of both her parents. I just can't imagine her taking on that acerbic tone of her husband's.

"When I take the whole picture of the Tucker I knew," he adds after a moment's consideration, "if I isolate one or two elements of it, I guess they do fit with the Tucker he's become. Though he could be the definition of glib, he always had an ease of speaking, and an ease of writing. It was not combined with trenchant insight — he wasn't somebody you thought would go all the way to Harvard and write books about James Joyce — but he wrote well. I didn't think he was going into literature. But there was a bit of a honey-tongue, and I think he was appreciated and enjoyed as amenable, upbeat, nice, and witty, especially by the popular group of kids. He had a gift for being articulate."

A more objective assessment might be that, for all the missteps along the way, it was at St. George's that Carlson began to fully come into his own as a singular and self-possessed individualist.

For instance, it was at St. George's that Tucker, otherwise not much interested in matters sartorial, began sporting the bow ties with which he would one day be associated.

Rushton pauses, then adds, seemingly as an afterthought, his voice a mix of disappointment and scorn: "But who becomes Tucker? Not many people."

Rushton mentions that several years ago, soon after he started at Fox, Carlson was in Birmingham and tried to track down his old English teacher. "He tried to get in touch with me," Rushton says, "he made some gesture. It was odd, and surprised me a little, because I already knew what his politics were. It was nice he tried to get in touch. But I'm a left-leaning Democrat, I don't like any of that crap at Fox."

Susie's parents, for their part, definitely did not approve of the relationship, repeatedly telling her Tucker was bad news. He had a reputation as a shit-stirrer; on a bulletin board reserved for announcements about athletics or tutoring, he would pin up editorials he wrote arguing against faculty decisions. And after joining the debate team junior year, he turned the club into a spectacle, with kids packing the room to watch, particularly after he started taking on teachers. "And, of course, he won every time," says Susie.

"A lot of people didn't like him, too," she allows, of her parents' hostility. "He was naughty, he wasn't a rule-follower. One of our closest friends once said you either hate him or love him, and that was true even then.

"There were kids then that really didn't like him. But my view was always that it was because he made them feel insecure because he's so self-confident. He genuinely doesn't care what other people think, which is very threatening to some people. And he would argue if he disagreed, and some people just can't handle that kind of confrontation. But he was never mean."

Too, behind the easy-to-read-as-cocky exterior, there was a quiet sensitivity. Thinking back on his time at St. George's, Tucker later describes in detail the trees lining the long drive leading to the campus. "They were incredible — mature but not dying, at peak awesomeness for a tree. I remember I'd drive down that driveway and just be overcome with the thought that *Wow, those trees have been there since the 1890s, when the school was founded.* They were planted by some forty-year-old, who probably died in the 1930s, when those trees were still sort of sad, and never saw them become what they are now. And I'd think: *Why did he do that?* He did it because he cared what people in the 1980s would think. And the force of that impulse just hit me — wanting to improve the lives of people you'll never meet. I still think about that. And I plant a lot of trees."

Just before graduation, Susie's parents sat her down in the living room for a talk. In no uncertain terms, she was told she could no longer see Tucker Carlson. "It was horrible," Susie recalls.

Later that week the family went to London for a vacation and, "I refused to talk to my parents the entire vacation. They would walk into a museum and I was always fifteen yards behind them the whole time, the entire ten days. I can be stubborn. It was bratty. But I was mad."

Ignoring her parents' diktat, she continued to date Tucker secretly through college. He was at Trinity College in Hartford, Connecticut, and Susie was a thousand miles away in Nashville, attending Vanderbilt, yet she managed to visit him regularly, with her parents still in the dark.

"You can't tell my wife what to do," Tucker tells me later, admiringly. "I've never tried. I'm not into telling people what to do anyway, but especially her. She won't fight you, she's just like, 'Nah. We're not doing that.' I said to her the other day, you've made it fifty-four years without doing anything you don't want to do, like *anything*. How'd you do that?" He laughs. "She got bossed around by her mother when she was little, she was sent to boarding school, but after that she said, 'I'm not doing anything I don't want to do, ever.' I'm not kidding. It's like trying to get a cat in a box, it's all paws!"

A love match from the start, by any standard, theirs has been a remarkably solid marriage. Tucker regularly makes the depth of his respect and admiration for Susie matter-of-factly apparent, and she is his most wholehearted supporter and defender. "It almost makes me cry," she'll tell me at one point, "that he can be so misunderstood. Because I truly don't know anyone as thoughtful and wise and enthusiastic and energetic, or anyone who enjoys other people more — the sheer joy of conversation and free exchange of ideas."

CHAPTER SEVEN

Tucker entered Trinity in 1987, the heart of the Reagan years, when America's campuses were seeing a sharp resurgence of student activism. A liberal-arts school with a student body of around seventeen hundred, Trinity wasn't an especially political place, but there were occasional protests even there.

Early on during Carlson's freshmen year, when the CIA came to campus to recruit, a group of leftist students objecting to their presence set up shop on the main quad, while a group of pro-CIA counter-protesters, mainly jocks, countered by unfurling a bedsheet spray-painted "Welcome CIA, out their dorm window directly above, as they blasted out the stirring patriotic address delivered by George C. Scott as Patton to drown out the protesters. In the ensuing chaotic back and forth, each side trying to score points over the din, the pro-CIA jocks looked around for a spokesman and someone handed Tucker the mic, imploring, "You speak for us, you're good!"

But, even then, Tucker was not about to be told what to say or how to say it.

He got on the stage and, as a friend who was there remembers, he "looked at the angry leftists on one side, and looked at the meathead pro-CIA guys on the other side, and said, 'If you want to know what I really think, I think you're all just a bunch of greasy chicken fuckers.'" The friend laughs. "No one was expecting that. But that's him, he's not a joiner. He was genuinely put off by the people protesting because he thought it was silly, and they were just doing it because kids were protesting at other schools. But he also wasn't going to sign up with people who wanted to shut them up and drown them out."

"He was the same way he is now," another college friend, Rev. Billy Cerveny, today a pastor in Nashville, Tennessee, told *Business Insider*. "He was a force of nature. He had a sense of presence and gravitas. You might get into an argument with him, but you end up loving the guy."

During the 1992 presidential election cycle, pitting Bill Clinton against GOP incumbent George H.W. Bush, Tucker touted third-party candidate Ross Perot to his friends — though it was hard for some of them to know how seriously to take him. As one classmate told *Business Insider*, he "liked the way Ross Perot was basically throwing a wrench into the system. He wasn't a serious Ross Perot proponent. He was cheering on somebody who was screwing up the system."

Neil Patel met Tucker Carlson "within about a half hour of us showing up to college. I went to see my buddy and they were in a four-person room, and Tucker was one of the four with him. We went and got drunk and proceeded to do the same thing for, you know, a few weeks."

The Indian-born Patel — publisher of the right-leaning news site the *Daily Caller*, which he founded with Carlson in 2009, after previously working as chief policy advisor to Vice President Dick Cheney — has been a close friend ever since.

After freshman year, with six or eight other buddies, the two of them moved to a duplex off-campus on Crescent Street, in a working-class section of Hartford. There were two front doors side-by-side, one onto the first floor and the other opening to a set of stairs leading to the second-floor unit. Each had three bedrooms and the guys converted other rooms in the units to sleeping quarters. Tucker lived on the front porch, which was enclosed by windows and not insulated. He hung sheets and towels to block out the light.

"I remember if he had a glass of water in the winter near his bed it would be frozen in the morning," Patel recalls. "He loved the porch, though. That was, like, his zone."

A prototypical bachelor pad, the house's furniture was festooned with cigarette holes; and the guys constructed two bars, one in the main living room and another in the attic.

But Tucker largely kept to himself in his cramped porch bedroom, where he'd constructed shelves to house his books. His father mailed him a stack of magazine and newspaper articles every few weeks. He grew out his hair, donned baggy clothes, studied the humanities, went to rock concerts, listened to his favorite band, the Grateful Dead, and drove a Volkswagen van.

Carlson decided to major in history. When his friends rushed a fraternity, Delta Phi, known as St. Elmo's, Tucker declined, but he ended up moving into their frat house senior year anyway.

"I remember explicitly him saying 'Look, I want to focus on what my faith is about and I thought this would be a big distraction,'" Rev. Cerveny recalls.

"Tucker and Susie had their moral compass pointing north even back then," another college friend told *Business Insider*. "Tucker's faith was not something he was focused on in his early years, but when he met Susie . . . that started to blossom and grow in him. Now it's a huge part of his life."

On visits to Trinity, Susie remembers Tucker as being "exactly the same" as he is today. "He was always a leader among his friends. He lived in a fraternity house but he refused to join the fraternity, because he's a total nonconformist. He wasn't all that interested in classes, but he would read everything. He was self-educated, totally," she says.

The summer following freshman year, Patel and Carlson spent two months in Central America, mostly Nicaragua, with shorter visits to Guatemala and Costa Rica. The Contra War was a hugely controversial issue at the time, with U.S.-backed Nicaraguan counterrevolutionary groups fighting the Marxist Sandinista government. "We were both pretty conservative, anti-communist," says Patel, "and were fascinated by what was going on down there."

Through Tucker's dad's connections with Voice of America, the two landed an internship, of sorts, at the main Contra newspaper, *La Prensa*. "Mostly we wandered around the country drinking and meeting interesting people. It was an amazing experience," Patel recalls. "It was a communist country. They were not used to American tourism. They certainly weren't used to *conservative* American kids going down there."

To the contrary, most young Americans who traveled to Nicaragua — including Bernie Sanders and future New York Mayor Bill de Blasio — were leftist activists enamored of the Marxist Sandinistas. While the long-haired and thoroughly grungy Patel and Carlson certainly looked the part, the Sandinista government marked them on arrival as supporters of the hated opposition. "They let us know early they were watching us," says Patel, recalling the time in a bar that a man seated nearby casually asked their ages. Sensing something might be up, Patel replied with a date off by a year, and "The guy corrected me. He made it absolutely clear they knew who we were."

Throughout the summer, the eighteen-year-old thrill-seekers, purportedly working as "reporters," yearned to be where the action was. They repeatedly tried to rendezvous with Contra fighters, but were never able to, only once reaching the general vicinity of the fighting.

Still, for both the experience was formative. "I saw firsthand the effect that communism had on the country," Patel says, "the poverty and the fear that a lot of people lived with down there."

During their junior year, the world was transfixed by the forthcoming Nicaraguan election pitting the Sandinista leader Daniel Ortega, who'd been in power since 1979, against right-wing challenger Violeta Chamorro, whose family owned *La Prensa*, the boys' nominal employer two years earlier.

Invited by Nicaraguan friends to return to the country for the big event, Patel and Tucker leapt at the chance, bringing along two friends who'd heard about their earlier escapades. Unsure of what to do when they showed up, they went to the press center and flashed their American driver's licenses as press credentials. It worked.

Across the room, Tucker spotted P.J. O'Rourke, the celebrated author and humorist, on hand to cover the election for *Rolling Stone*. Tucker was a big fan, having devoured his books and columns in *The American Spectator.*

Moreover, O'Rourke was accompanied by another conservative superstar, the renegade leftist David Horowitz, and, says Patel, "those guys were so tickled that these American conservative kids who looked like hippies had snuck into the press center and were hanging out and trying to find action at the election, they took us under their wing and brought us everywhere."

When Chamorro won, Carlson and Patel were there at her rapturous victory party.

Chamorro, still alive today at ninety-seven, would serve as Nicaragua's president until 1997; Ortega, now seventy-seven, would regain power in 2007, and remains president today.

Thirty three years later, sitting in the kitchen of his winter home on Florida's Gulf Coast, I ask Carlson how that experience shaped his understanding of politics.

He hesitates — just waking up, he's wearing a pair of boxer shorts and the blue-and-white gingham shirt he wore on television last night — and he considers a moment, before responding. For him, the question, and the memory, carry unexpected implications.

"I would say the takeaway for me, long-term, which really did help form the basis and thinking about everything," he begins, in a gravelly voice, "is the closer you get to something, the more confusing it tends to become, and the more you realize you don't understand, and the more the distinctions between the good guys and bad guys become blurry.

"Ortega was an absolute thug. He was completely dictatorial, completely utilitarian, and had secret police and political prisons and killed his opponents. He had super bad supporters.

"But Ortega turned out to be one of the only leaders in the world who didn't buy the Covid lockdowns. He's a Marxist authoritarian. He executed his political prisoners. You expect him to jump on Covid immediately as a pretext. No, just the opposite. Nicaragua became a haven for people who didn't want the vaccine, didn't want lockdowns. Libertarian left, right, freedom-minded hippies, all kinds of different groups who didn't buy into the Covid authoritarianism moved to Nicaragua during the pandemic. Friends of mine moved to Nicaragua, and they aren't liberal at all, they voted for Trump. Explain that to me. It's just incredible." He pauses. "It's like getting a text from Naomi Wolf saying, 'Thank you for what you're doing.' What? Naomi Wolf, the feminist?

"So then, there's a point in every honest man's life when you realize, I'm just too old to understand this. All I can do is enjoy it. And, luckily, I don't need to understand it, I'm just calling it as I see it."

He tells me he was even more befuddled to learn, a couple years ago, that the left-wing dictator of Venezuela, Nicolás Maduro, was a "mega-fan" of his show, and wanted to meet him.

"I have a friend who is a lifelong, crazy Marxist — and this person is friends with Nicolás Maduro, and he said, 'They love you, he watches your show every night.' I don't really know what's happening there, it seems really bad. They're eating zoo animals, right? Every Venezuelan has lost like twenty pounds due to starvation. I don't think I support that. It bothered me. I didn't ask any follow-up questions, because I didn't want to know." He laughs.

"So I just put that into my large and growing file of weird phenomena that means something, but I'm not sure what it means. UFOs are in there. Naomi Wolf becoming someone I agree with, I don't know what that means, either. That's in that file. But that file, the 'to be determined' file in my head, adds at this point to my only analysis that things are changing in a really, really deep way. Not in a bullshit way. Not in a 'Oh, more Hispanics are voting for Trump,' shallow way, but there's actually some huge changes underway the outlines of which are unknown to me."

Tucker has made abundantly clear over the years that he has little use for politicians, right, left, or in between. But he's found one even he can get behind, at least for now: Nayib Bukele, the forty-one-year-old president of El Salvador. The smallest nation in Central America and once the murder capital of the Western hemisphere, El Salvador has undergone a sweeping metamorphosis since Bukele was elected in 2019, and declared a state of emergency against the gang violence that once plagued the nation. Since the crackdown, liberal American media like *The New York Times* and CNN — the same outlets that relentlessly pushed Covid-19 lockdowns and mandatory vaccinations — have fretted over Bukele's "dangerous bargain of sacrificing civil liberties for safety," but at home he enjoys a 90 percent approval rating.

After Bukele appeared on Carlson's evening show, he invited him to Maine to film an hour of *Tucker Carlson Today*. It was partridge season and Bukele didn't even know what a partridge was, but with the Salvadoran's large security contingent in tow, the two went tromping off into the woods. Tucker later shows me a picture of them side by side in hunting gear, Carlson holding his childhood shotgun.

"It's very easy to create a binary from a distance between good and evil," he adds now, "these are our allies, these are our enemies. But that's only possible at a distance, just like anything, just like a marriage. You know, many, many, many times in my life, including this week, I've talked to people about their marriages, I give people advice on a marriage and the first round of conversations, you always have a really clear picture about who's right and who's wrong. Then the deeper you get into it, you realize it's actually this kind of very messy mixture of responsibility for the disaster. It's never as clear as you think it is, ever, because people are just very complicated, super complicated. The more you know the more you realize you don't know what motivates people.

"I learned that interviewing criminals. I've interviewed a lot in writing about crime, interviewed a lot of people convicted of horrifying crimes — rapes, murder. And there's no excuse for murder. I'm not trying to construct an excuse. But you get into it, and it's like the motives are always different from what we think they were.

"And everything is more complicated than you think it is, including and especially in wars. I learned that because the Cold War was the most easy story to analyze. It was, like, the atheist communist country versus the West. It wasn't hard for me and I still feel that way. Living in Washington as a kid, my dad was working for the government and was very engaged in the Cold War, and that feud was a defining feature of my childhood.

"However, the war between the Contras and the Sandinistas was just more complicated than that. Because it was a civil war, it's never really about ideology. It's about ideology, plus long-standing blood feuds, plus economics, plus . . . there's just a lot of different things going on. Plus, of course, it's always a proxy between two larger powers. And that was the first time I thought, wow, this is actually quite complex."

He momentarily pauses again. "The Ukrainian and Russian conflict is effectively a civil war. These are like siblings fighting each other. So, it becomes a proxy for a larger power struggle and that was absolutely the case in Nicaragua.

"That, to me, is the beginning of the beginning of wisdom: realizing the limits of wisdom. And the limits of your understanding and the limits of what's knowable and all that."

CHAPTER
EIGHT

Although listed in Trinity's class of 1992, Carlson never graduated college. He didn't have the credits, and he didn't receive a diploma.

This was, and remains, a matter of complete unconcern to his father. "Really?" Dick replies when I ask him about it. "I was under the impression that he did, but maybe he didn't. I guess it hasn't made much of a difference."

Tucker says simply: "School was over, I wasn't going to graduate, and I was getting married. I was, like, I want to get the fuck out of this place. Same with Susie."

Over the decades since, Tucker has found no reason to regret that choice — quite the contrary — and of course is also keenly aware of how even more useless (and actively destructive) academia is today. As he laughingly told a conference of the conservative student group Turning Point USA, he is constantly offending contemporaries with college-age kids by saying so. They are "completely vested in the symbols of attainment of achievement, which don't actually connote real attainment or achievement. . . . (T)he goal of everybody my age is like 'Hayden's at Duke — he got into Penn, but we just felt like Duke was better.' There's no reference at all to what Hayden is *learning* at Duke, which is nothing. He's being taught to hate America, hate his parents, hate the system that made Duke possible. . ."

The truth is, he continued, "there's no fixing this. . . . I mean, if you're going to drill my bicuspids, I want you to go to dental school. I'm not against education, but the liberal arts, a communications degree from Penn State, I'm sorry, it will be worth nothing. You're going to be deeply indebted, and there's a very good chance it will hurt you . . .

"One of the big lies of higher education is you can go to school and learn something for which you have no basic aptitude. And that's a total lie. You could send me for twenty years of MIT and I would never understand physics. I just wouldn't, I can't do math. I'm dyslexic, done. Do the thing for which you're naturally suited. Pay attention to who you are. Do the thing that you are naturally good at, that you love without being prompted, that you would do for free, that's totally true. Don't lie to yourself."

That summer, with their classmates in graduation fervor, Tucker and Susie — who had similarly quit Vanderbilt early — were in Potsdam, New York, near the Canadian border. Stopping into a local drug store, they saw graduation gowns for rent.

Carlson one evening shows me a photo of the two twenty-two-year-olds snapped by a passerby, standing on a sidewalk, mock-proudly posing in the rented gowns. "I was half drunk," says Tucker.

"I was half drunk all the time." He points. "I still have those tennis shoes."

Then, laughing: "It was Susie's idea. She's so demented. My wife is actually extremely subversive, even in some ways more than I am. She's the nicest person in the world, but deep down she's got a spirit of go-fuck-yourself. Big time. And I respect that. It's not a point of conflict among us at all. It's a subject of admiration. I wish I was more like that. And she's super beautiful and she's super involved with her children, she likes all that. When she had our first baby — I'm making like $29,000 a year at the time — she goes back to work, and then comes home and says, 'No, I'm not doing that.' I hadn't grown up in a traditional family, so I had no expectations — does a wife work? Does a mother work? I don't know. But she decided that's not for her, and she never went back."

Before they could get married, Carlson requested his father's permission — which he readily received — but of course Susie's father's permission was far more in doubt; he was unaware the two had been an item for nearly six years.

Susie decided the best way through to her dad was via her mother, who'd always been the more disapproving parent. At home during Thanksgiving, she took her mom out to Chili's.

"I'll never forget it," she says. "We're sitting at the bar and we've ordered drinks and I say, 'Mom I need to talk to you about something. Tucker Carlson and I have been dating and we want to get married.' I had to use his last name because I didn't think she'd even remember who he was. And as I said it, the waitress walks past and my mom turns to her and says, 'I'd like another margarita.'"

Susie offers a rather pained smile at the memory.

But the tension was broken, and Susie soon won her mom over. So Tucker then had to take Susie's father out to lunch, which, she says, proved a relative snap. "Pop was like, 'of course. That's great. I just want you to have a job.'"

Her parents even paid for a two-week Bermuda honeymoon — though, eager to get started on their real life, Tucker and Susie didn't stay the whole two weeks. "We've been in four years of college," says Susie, "our entire life has been a vacation . . ."

Tucker had always wanted to be a journalist. "Journalists were proud to be open-minded," as he wrote in 2001," and I was proud to become one. My father was a reporter, and he embodied everything I associated with journalism. He was smart, curious, and relentlessly skeptical. It was impossible to bullshit my father. No one told journalists what to say. Reporters were free men, and they lived like it. If they could prove it, they could write it. Period. That was the whole point of belonging to a class specifically protected by the Bill of Rights."

Even better, at the time, before the field became so deeply politicized and writers were free to pursue stories not straitjacketed by the approved narrative, the profession still called forth glamor and romance. "I wrote magazine stories for decades, long after I went into television and no longer needed the $600," Tucker would later reflect. "I did it because it was interesting. In order to produce a decent magazine piece, you had to go places, meet people, see unusual things. It was an adventure every time."

Returning home from their honeymoon, Tucker quickly landed a starter job as assistant editor at *Policy Review*, the quarterly publication for the conservative think tank the Heritage Foundation, and the young couple found a house in the Georgetown section of Washington, D.C.

Tucker's job, which paid $14,000 a year, at first mainly involved fact-checking articles by phone. To make things more interesting, he also appointed himself "nut-mail editor," going through letters that more senior staffers had no time for, often sent by those upset by something they'd seen in the magazine or, just as likely, pushing some conspiracy theory. "It started out as fun," he later wrote, "but even nut mail gets boring if you read enough of it. To keep myself amused, I began writing back. Baiting crazies is a mean thing to do — even at the time I recognized that. But I couldn't help myself. So I assured the mad scientist in Baltimore that his Alternative Theory of Gravity really did make sense. I told a number of framed-by-the-Man prison inmates that we'd begin investigations into their cases. And I stoked countless conspiracy theories."

At last given the opportunity to write for the magazine, he took full advantage. In 1995 he published a nine-thousand-word article — exhaustive by magazine standards — titled "How to Close Down a Crack House in Your Neighborhood." In the course of researching it, Carlson interviewed drug addicts and tagged along with a community organizer named Herman Wrice and his group, in their signature white hard hats, through Philadelphia's blighted Mantua neighborhood. Like carolers, they stopped outside crack houses in the neighborhood, singing "drugs are no good," in order to deter dealers and junkies from going inside.

It was clear even then that Carlson had a gift for long-form journalism, one that would eventually be recognized by editors from a range of mainstream publications. Like many young writers, he was drawn to subjects that were challenging and sometimes, in the reporting, grueling.

In *Policy Review* he soon published another sprawling report, this one on the impact of Christian prison-fellowships in lowering rates of recidivism, even as he simultaneously labored on a book, eventually abandoned, on community crime control.

"I was impressed by the quality of his mind," former *Policy Review* editor Adam Meyerson told the *Washington Post* in 1999. "We talked about C.S. Lewis, Whittaker Chambers, Nicaragua, and he had a contagious enthusiasm about ideas. He had a real nose for news and a crack prose style."

Still, Carlson yearned for greater adventure and a more unconventional life. In 1992 he left Washington and headed to Little Rock, Arkansas, where he'd landed a job as a reporter for the *Arkansas Democrat-Gazette.* He and Susie had not yet had children, and she was working as a religion teacher in a private school in Virginia. She stayed behind for three months to finish out the school year before joining her husband.

"One thing I love about Susie, and I'm so grateful for, is she is literally up for anything. Fucking anything! I love it," Tucker says. "I come home from work one day and I say, I got this job offer from a newspaper in Arkansas. And I really want to work at a newspaper. I feel a moral obligation to work at a newspaper. *The Washington Post* won't hire me. My dad worked at the *L.A. Times.* If you want to be a journalist, you need newspaper experience. She's from Grosse Point, Michigan and the Northeast, she doesn't know Arkansas. And I ask her, 'Will you move to Arkansas with me?'" he says.

"Of course!" Susie replied, followed by, "Is that near Colorado?"

"I'll never forget that," Carlson laughs.

Carlson needed to find a place to live. "I have incredibly low standards. I'll sleep on the floor. I have no problem sleeping in my car. I've done it a thousand times. I have very low sanitary and comfort standards, I've always been that way. I don't care. I shave with soap. I'm that guy," Carlson says. His father saw around the corner. "Remember, she's a woman. She has different standards than you. Please don't fuck her over," he told his son.

Taking his father's advice, Carlson found what he thought was a beautiful two-bedroom apartment. It was in a complex; there was a laundry room in a separate hut in the middle of a courtyard. It was $212.50 a month.

"I go into the office and there's this lady literally smoking with the door closed, air conditioning on, smoking menthols," he says. "I paid my $212 deposit and got this depressing but spacious apartment and I didn't even notice who else was in the apartment complex. So, I'm pretty psyched. And I call Susie and tell her how great it is, it's awesome, we can even get a dog."

Susie arrives. Turns out, the complex was Section Eight housing. "She grew up in fairly nice circumstances, but she'll roll with anything," Carlson says. "It was bad. It was so bad. No one worked. Like, everyone's grandson was living there. She'd walk to the laundry and there'd be some guy hanging out drinking beer out of a bottle, like 'Hey baby.' Boy, she was mad! But I made us stay for six months so I could get my $212 deposit back."

From there they moved to a small $600-a-month house on Greenwood Road in Little Rock's Cammack Village neighborhood. "The whole culture of Arkansas was so different from anything I'd ever experienced before. The whole state is run by, like, six families. You have hugely rich people in Arkansas, a relatively small middle class, for America, and then hillbillies and poor black people in the Delta. It was crazy. I'd never lived in a hierarchical society before. I'd lived in America before, which was not hierarchical, it wasn't then, it is now. I'm from California, which was the biggest middle class in the world. We were pretty affluent, but we weren't living on another planet. We ate at Denny's, everybody did. We ate at McDonald's all the time. It was just a less stratified world. Arkansas was stratified. I'd never seen anything like it. It was like living in Mexico, being in Monterrey and your family owns Tecate Beer and you have servants who grovel around and you go to the club with all other rich people. It was crazy," says Carlson.

Susie got a job as a teacher at an upscale private preschool. Despite being young and broke and seeing themselves as on the lowest rung on the totem pole, they were invited into Little Rock society and granted membership to the country club, owing to a connection at the newspaper. "I don't play golf, but I could see myself having brunch on the veranda like it was the country club in Nairobi in 1920," he laughs. "But we really enjoyed it. It was a very interesting job and I just liked the culture. I'd never lived in the South before. I didn't really understand it at all, but I liked it."

He recalls one afternoon when Susie had a meeting with the headmistress of the school where she taught, "the classic kind of headmistress, a local society woman, wonderful manners." The woman, in her sixties, had to cancel abruptly. She called Susie that morning to say her husband, who was at a duck camp for the month over in Stuttgart, an hour east of Little Rock, was coming home for a couple hours because he had needs, and so the meeting would have to be postponed.

"I was, like, what? Her husband's horny, so he calls up his wife from duck camp and she cancels the rest of her day?" Carlson laughs. "'Yeah, I shot my limit this morning. Be home at noon, baby!'" Susie thought it was disgusting. "Susie was freaked out about how much I enjoyed that. I was like, this is the greatest thing I've ever heard."

During his first week in Little Rock, Tucker got a speeding ticket. A colleague wondered why Carlson didn't show the officer his press pass. "Oh, no, we don't pay speeding tickets. We're the newspaper. Just put it in an envelope and send it to this judge." Carlson was flabbergasted. "It was amazing. I grew up in a world where no one cheated on anything. There was no inside way to do anything in California in the Seventies and Eighties. Everyone paid the same. This was like an offense against Anglo culture, that some people get to cut to the head of the line," he says.

"D.C. is totally like that," observes Tucker, "but because I didn't grow up like that, when we were living there for a time I resisted it. But ultimately after thirty years in D.C. we just embraced it and got a fixer and all of our problems went away. D.C. is just so corrupt. I'm an egalitarian. I don't like that."

During Tucker's Little Rock stint, former Arkansas Governor Bill Clinton was in the White House, and it's not hard to argue that to a remarkable degree he imposed his hometown's flexible, free-and-easy moral standards on the entire country.

Indeed, the Clintons' noxious influence on the nation and its values would go far beyond the legitimization of Dogpatch shenanigans and run-of-the-mill grift.

"The Clintons were small-timers, for sure," says Carlson. "they were coming from a very insular political culture. But they changed not just Washington, but the world by making it okay for liberals to worship money. All of a sudden you could be, quote, 'liberal' and still make a billion dollars as a rapacious capitalist, as long as you made the right noises about some liberation movement or global warming. That had not been allowed before the Clintons. George McGovern was not encouraging people to go into banking, and very few people who voted for George McGovern did go into banking, because George McGovern was suspicious of the banks. Bernie Sanders was the last living specimen of that wing of the Democratic Party, where Democratic politicians did not suck up to oligarchs, at least in public. They sucked up to labor leaders and civil-rights leaders and the common man, the people without power.

"But during those eight years of Clinton, it changed. He was the cheerleader for the tech boom which, of course, exploded the second he left office. He'd say the tech titans were the heroes, and I remember thinking: *This is amazing, this is definitely not the liberalism I grew up with*. But that's where woke capitalism started, under Bill Clinton. You could still tell your kids you're a Democrat, you're a liberal, you're progressive, you're a *good person*, even when you're participating in and benefiting from the biggest wealth transfer in human history from the middle class to the top one percent. So as income stratification grows more and more unstable, the rich still get to tell themselves they're good people in a way that, say, Andrew Carnegie never could.

Andrew Carnegie actually had to prove it by building stone libraries in hundreds of towns across the country — by actually, giving back. He had no choice if he wanted to continue living in this country, because people understood that when you're accumulating that much wealth — even by admirable industry and innovation — by definition you are doing it at somebody else's expense. There are *losers.* And if you're becoming so disproportionately wealthy and powerful in what at that time was still a pretty egalitarian country, someone was paying the bill, and you must, in some sense, atone for it.

"But the problem with giving back is it's expensive. So under Clinton the oligarchs realized, 'Wait a second, we can do this without getting picketed at our homes.' We'll be totally fine as long as we support trans rights and Zelenskyy.

"I get picketed at home just for calling out the oligarchs, but nobody's organizing a campaign against Jeff Bezos for totally destroying retail." He laughs. "There was a time, it wasn't that long ago, when the Democratic Party was organized around hassling big business for higher pay and better benefits for workers, who were Democrats. When was the last time you heard that Walmart was bad because they don't offer health insurance? Walmart is more woke than Oberlin College.

"There has never been a more destructive alignment than the one we currently see between big business and the kind of radical theoretical Left in the universities. Companies like The Gap, or MasterCard, or Citibank will take some bizarre new talking point about trans rights, or trans humanism, or whatever ugly, stupid poisonous concept is emerging from the universities, and they'll defang it and incorporate it into ad campaigns, and then they'll continue to pay a much lower tax rate than you do, and nobody says anything.

"Big companies have always had a lot of power because that's where the money was, but they never before had moral power. But once they donned the cloak of moral superiority, there was no fighting them. Apple gets to sell its products at ruinous prices that most Americans can't afford — $1,000 for an iPhone. How many kids in the low-income zip codes have them? Everybody. How does that work? What percentage of their monthly income are they spending on that iPhone and the service plan? That's a great question but, of course, it's never asked. If Apple really wanted to make the world better, it would make a $30 iPhone. It could, but it won't.

"That all started under Clinton and that was more destructive than maybe anything anybody's ever done as president."

CHAPTER NINE

T ucker and Susie remained in Arkansas for a year and a half. But when Rupert Murdoch launched *The Weekly Standard* in 1995, Tucker lobbied everyone he knew for a job there, and the Carlsons moved back to Washington.

At the upstart conservative magazine, Tucker soon carved out the writerly personage of a jaunty nuisance thrown into absurd and incredible situations, a gonzo style reminiscent of his early inspiration, Hunter S. Thompson. He soon became sought after for long-form and narrative political writing in both conservative and mainstream publications.

"He's great at digging up stuff and great at getting people to confide in him and tell him things they later wish they hadn't," Bill Kristol, *The Weekly Standard*'s editor, told *The Washington Post* in 1999. "He's engaging and boyish, and people take a liking to him." Kristol went on to say, "Some Republicans and conservatives think he's a fellow conservative and he'll give them a break. Tucker, to his credit, reports it like it is."

In a blurb for Carlson's 2003 book *Politicians, Partisans, and Parasites*, Kristol wrote, "Tucker Carlson is neither a smooth-talking politician, nor a rabid partisan, nor a cloying parasite. He is a witty writer and a skilled storyteller. Read his book, laugh out loud, and learn a lot about TV, Washington, D.C., and life."

Kristol — who would go on to be the standard-bearer for Never Trumpers, the neoconservatives bitterly (and often viciously) opposed to the populist, Trumpian shift in the Republican Party, now feels rather differently about his onetime protégé. In his obsessive tweeting about Carlson, Kristol regularly veers into lunatic territory, describing Tucker as a pawn of Russian President Vladimir Putin and suggesting, for example, that "those who knew or know him should stop referring to Tucker Carlson as 'Tucker,' as if he's a friendly acquaintance. 'Carlson' will do. Like 'Riefenstahl.'"

Kristol did not respond to a request to be interviewed for this book.

Carlson's 1996 profile of political strategist James Carville in *The Weekly Standard* shows him at the height of his form. The "populist plutocrat," as Carlson termed his subject, is portrayed as at once reptilian and opportunistic and completely charming; in short, as the sort of complicated human beings most writers are loath to flesh out, particularly in politically oriented publications. "What I discovered in talking to him was that James Carville was indeed a fraud, but openly so, in the most honest and genuine way," he would later observe. "Over time, Carville wound up one of my favorite people in the world, one of the few friends I've gone to repeatedly for serious life advice. I haven't taken a new job in twenty years without calling him first. James Carville is a genuinely wise man."

In 1997, Carlson became involved in what Washington gossip types would remember as a legendary feud with conservative activist and lobbyist Grover Norquist. In a piece for the *New Republic*, Carlson blasted Norquist for lobbying on behalf of the Marxist government of the Seychelles, where Tucker's father had been ambassador, reportedly making $10,000 a month. Norquist had once publicly opposed the regime, and Carlson called it "A remarkably cynical reversal . . . Norquist sounds like any other cash-addled, morally malleable lobbyist in Washington." He later called Norquist "repulsive," and a "mean-spirited, humorless, dishonest little creep . . . an embarrassing anomaly, the leering, drunken uncle everyone else wishes would stay home."

Norquist made his fight against Tucker also one against his father, at the time president of the Corporation for Public Broadcasting, by enlisting his Americans for Tax Reform organization in the battle to defund public broadcasting, and awarding Dick its "Enemy of the Taxpayer" award. Norquist also reportedly lobbied Rupert Murdoch to defund *The Weekly Standard*.

The feud exploded into the tabloids after Carlson one evening "accidentally" spilled a full glass of Bloody Mary over Norquist's head. "The celery stuck behind Grover's ear, making him look like a conservative Carmen Miranda," one source told the *New York Post*. A colleague of Norquist's then chased Carlson down and threw a glass of wine in his face.

By 2011, when the two appeared side-by-side at a Republican National Committee debate, the ill feeling appeared to have been smoothed over. "We never had any differences," Carlson told the

Washington Examiner, with "a knowing smile." "Not that I would ever admit to. I don't recall that. I have no idea what you're talking about."

In a 1998 report for the Manhattan Institute's *City Journal,* Carlson wrote knowingly of the politics shaping the Republican party ahead of the 2000 election. "Two of the highest-polling contenders for the Republican nomination, Gov. George W. Bush of Texas and Sen. John Ashcroft of Missouri, are likely to conduct campaigns based on resurrecting the traditional morality that the '60s rejected," he observed approvingly, noting that while Bill Clinton was the poster boy of the destructive, self-indulgent ethos of the '60s, Bush and Ashcroft gave speech after speech lauding the virtues of responsibility, self-control, and restoring the culture to greatness. For both men, "the '60s offered no fulfillment of American ideals of liberty and creativity, but cultural breakdown."

Rarely had he written anything so obviously heartfelt.

Assigned the following year to profile Republican presidential nominee George W. Bush for Tina Brown's newly-launched *Talk* magazine, he portrayed the soon-to-be president as a likable, if mildly boneheaded and easily distracted, frat boy. The Bush campaign was furious that Carlson repeatedly quoted Bush using the word "fuck"; and even more upset by his inclusion of Bush's ridiculing of a female Texas death-row inmate, Karla Faye Tucker, who, convicted of murdering two people during a burglary, had unsuccessfully sought clemency from the Texas governor. Carlson described how, discussing the case, Bush, "his lips pursed in mock desperation," imitated the doomed woman, whispering "'Please . . . don't kill me.'"

"Mr. Carlson misread, mischaracterized me," claimed Bush afterward, clearly eager to stay on the good side of both Tucker and his influential magazine. "He's a good reporter, he just misunderstood about how serious that was. I take the death penalty very seriously. I take each case seriously. I just felt he misjudged me. I think he misinterpreted my feelings. I know he did."

A couple years ago the Carlsons attended a dinner party near their Florida home, at which the Bushes turned out to be the only other guests. This was more than a little awkward, as Tucker, while a Fox News host, had not been kind to Bush's older brother Jeb, in contrast to his often favorable take on the Bush clan's Public Enemy Number One, Donald Trump, who'd savaged "Low Energy Jeb" in 2016.

Except Tucker doesn't do awkward. Or if he does, he is likely to play it for laughs.

When they sat down for dinner, Carlson turned to George W. and told him he wanted to clear the air and apologize for their recent misgivings.

"I said to him, 'Look, I'm sorry about the whole Trump thing. I was caught up in the moment, I was completely misled. I don't know what I was thinking. Because, did you know, Trump *supports* abortion? Can you imagine actually supporting abortion?" Tucker howls recalling the moment. "You know, because the Bushes are the most pro-abortion people alive."

In a 2021 *GQ* hit piece on Carlson — by that point, there was no other kind — Tina Brown, the editor who'd commissioned the Bush piece for *Talk* (and is renowned as the onetime editor of *Vanity Fair* and *The New Yorker*, as well as the creator of the far-left *Daily*

Beast), recalled Carlson as "a fantastic writer . . . I thought he had the makings of a top talent."

Indeed, the issue of *Talk* magazine featuring the George W. Bush piece not only sold out on newsstands across the country, but endeared Carlson to many Democrats and a raft of liberal magazine editors, in some of whose good graces he would remain until the era of Trump.

Ironically, Carlson had first worried the Bush profile was too fluffy. "The night before I filed the story, I gave a copy to my wife," he later wrote. "Her one question after she'd finished reading it was, 'Aren't people going to think you're looking for a job in his administration?'"

The Weekly Standard then assigned him to cover Bush's rival for the GOP nomination, John McCain, and Carlson traveled with the candidate to New Hampshire, Michigan, Missouri, California, and, later, to Vietnam. While trying to board a flight with McCain in Ho Chi Minh City, Tucker was detained by the communist authorities, who claimed he was in the country illegally — apparently the result of someone having failed to stamp his passport on his arrival in the country. A smiling functionary in khaki with red stars on the epaulets and lacquered fingernails was interrogating Carlson when McCain walked over. "He's only smiling because he's got you," the former longtime resident of the Hanoi Hilton whispered to Carlson, drily.

What he needed to do, the supervisor instructed, was re-enter Vietnam so as to receive the entry stamp that hadn't been applied the first time. Of course, bureaucracy being what it is — and a communist bureaucracy at that — there was no way for him to get out so he could get back in.

Meanwhile McCain's caravan had to move on, with Tucker left behind. Powerful editors stateside were called upon, and CNN lobbied Bill Clinton's State Department, which issued a statement, but it was two days before the Vietnamese finally let him go. "I hate the phrase 'Kafkaesque,'" he said, safely back on American soil, "but it kind of was . . . I don't like to have some little fucking guy yelling at me. Plus, that language is such an ugly little language: 'Oh! Bow bow bow!'"

In the profile, McCain is portrayed as good-humored — "a happy warrior, maybe the only real one in American politics," — but also foolhardy, and personally unsure of himself and his abilities. It stood in dramatic contrast to the standard reports of journalists on the McCain beat, who invariably described the candidate as incomparably cool.

Carlson would later write that, in fact, his assessment of McCain had been too kind, for he'd failed to recognize the man's "flashes of ugliness" and "dark side," that would subsequently be apparent in the ways he later "disgraced himself with nastiness and dishonesty."

It is a measure of the notice he was generating that, in 2000, the messy-haired, bow-tied Carlson was being lauded in *People* magazine, of all places, as "conservatism's bright young wit." Moreover — something beyond inconceivable in today's toxic America — his byline was welcome in publications across the political spectrum.

In 2007, for instance, the leftist *New Republic* published his memorable profile of the libertarian maverick congressman Ron Paul, at the time campaigning for the GOP presidential nomination.

"Paul never outshines his message, which is unchanging: Let adults make their own choices; liberty works," he observed. "For a unified theory of everything, it's pretty simple. And Paul sincerely believes it. Most Republicans, of course, profess to believe it too. But only Paul has introduced a bill to legalize unpasteurized milk. Give yourself five minutes and see if you can think of a more countercultural idea than that.

"It's hard to think of a presidential candidate who's ever drawn a coalition as broad as Ron Paul's. At any Paul event, you're likely to run into self-described anarcho-capitalists, 9/11-deniers, antiwar lefties, objectivists, paleocons, hemp activists, and geeky high school kids, along with tax resisters, conspiracy nuts, and acolytes of Murray Rothbard. And those are just the ones it's possible to categorize. It's hard to say what they all have in common, except that every one is an ideological minority — or, as one of them put it to me, 'open-minded people.' To these supporters, Paul is a folk hero, the one person in national politics who doesn't judge them, who understands what it's like to be considered a freak by straight society."

It almost sounds like he's talking about his own future audience — and himself.

But the piece stands out, too, stylistically, highlighting a take on the world, an eye for telling detail, and a sneaking sympathy for social misfits clearly influenced by mentors like Hunter S. Thompson and P.J. O'Rourke.

At one point he writes of phoning a friend while trailing Paul in Nevada to ask if he'd like to tag along to a Ron Paul event. The friend was Dennis Hof, owner of the Moonlite BunnyRanch, the most famous legal brothel in the country.

"I wasn't planning on showing up at Paul's press conference with a bordello owner and two hookers," he explained, "but unexpected things happen on the road." One of the hookers, named Air Force Amy, wanted a picture with Paul, so after the candidate's press conference, Carlson led her to a back room where he was giving interviews.

"Dressed in red, her Dolly Parton hairdo and 36DDs at full attention, she sidled up to Lew Moore, Paul's campaign manager, and made her pitch," Carlson wrote. "'Hi,' she said. 'I'm Air Force Amy, and I'd like a picture with Ron Paul.' I knew right away it wasn't going to happen. 'I've got a concern, I've got to be honest,' Moore said, tense but trying to be nice. [...] I really thought Air Force Amy was going to cry. She looked crushed. Like a child of alcoholic parents, she immediately started to rationalize away the pain. 'It wasn't Ron's decision,' she told Moore. 'It was yours. So I can't take it personally.' But it was obvious that she did. It was awful."

Rare in political writers then, and unheard of today, the piece highlighted his own openness to different ideas and perspectives. Carlson describes how at first, hearing "Paul talk about monetary policy, I'd felt like a hostage, the only person in the room who didn't buy into the program. Then, slowly, like so many hostages, I started to open my mind and listen. By the time we got to Reno, unfamiliar thoughts were beginning to occur: Why shouldn't we worry about the soundness of the currency? What exactly is the dollar backed by anyway? And, if the gold standard is crazy, is it really any crazier than hedge funds? I'd become Patty Hearst, ready to take up arms for the cause, or at least call my accountant and tell him to buy Krugerrands."

Indeed, a large part of Tucker's appeal was his convention-defying unpredictability in both words and action. Once, as he was tooling down the road in his 1987 Volvo beside a reporter doing a profile on *him*, the reporter observed that his seatbelt was "defiantly unbuckled."

"I have to wear it? That's insane!" Tucker launched into a rant, pounding on the steering wheel for emphasis. "I'm pro-seat belt in the abstract. I just can't rise above the authority issue. It's my car!"

Carlson was once actually granted permission from the Department of Transportation to remove the airbags from another of his cars, a 1998 Chevy Suburban.

What his liberal admirers of course could not appreciate was that such displays weren't merely for show. Like his father, he despises the nanny state to the core of his being.

Dick, for his part, once described being flagged down by a frantic lifeguard while swimming off a Cape Cod beach with a snorkel and goggles. Why? Wearing a snorkel and mask in the water had been declared illegal, on the grounds that someone floating in the water with a mask and snorkel might be mistaken by the lifeguards as dead. "Three hundred years of governance," wrote Dick disgustedly in his memoir, "and it has come to this idiotic finish."

Another time, shopping for butter at the market he'd patronized for decades near their summer home in Maine, Dick approached the counter with his customary single stick, only to be told he was now obliged to buy a full pound. Why? There was a new law mandating "Nutrition Facts" be printed on all butter sold, and the wax papered individual sticks did not carry the information. Dick sarcastically asked if he could read the nutrition facts aloud from the pound package, then buy the single stick. No. Well, what if he wrote the nutrition information down and took it home with him? Uh uh. Maybe he could memorize and then recite the cholesterol, sodium, and fat content each time he came in? No.

Holding his ground, Dick left the store without any butter for his pancakes the next morning.

So no one can say Tucker doesn't come by it honestly. Like his father, he gets fired up by the government acting as national babysit-ter. And, for him, nothing is more representative of the appalling trend than the war on tobacco.

Carlson started smoking when he was thirteen, and by the mid-Nineties, writing for magazines, he was up to more than two packs of Camels a day. He only quit when he started working in the rarefied atmosphere of television, where the habit was more aggressively frowned upon, not only by colleagues but, now that his was a public face, by an increasingly large segment of the general public.

"Suddenly, the dynamic was different," he wrote, early on in his TV career. "People who recognized me from television always seemed stunned when they saw me smoking in public. The disapproval was too strong. They sounded shocked and deeply disappointed, like I'd been arrested for doing something creepy in a men's room. They treated me like Pee Wee Herman. . . . Weary of the battle, I surren-dered and allowed the dark forces of Health to claim victory over my personal life."

Until recently, eagle-eyed Fox viewers might have caught a glimpse of a tin of Zyn — an oral nicotine pouch placed in the mouth like chewing tobacco – on his desk when the camera captured a certain angle. He pops the stuff all day long.

On one broadcast in January 2023, at the close of a week that had seen another record-breaking number of illegals crossing into the U.S., a new batch of classified documents discovered in President

Joe Biden's possession, and Russia amping up threats of nuclear war over the conflict in Ukraine, Carlson opened his Friday show with an impassioned monologue addressing the Biden administration's threats to ban gas stoves.

"It turns out that liberals are very eager to intrude as deeply as possible into people's personal lives just as long as they control the government. Once they were in charge, they set about doing this with no limits and no acknowledgment of the existence of personal liberty," he said, going on to rail against mask mandates; the proposed 95 percent tax on cigars in New York; bans on menthol cigarettes ("some people like them, particularly poor people. They don't have a lot of pleasures, menthol cigarettes are one of them. But they can't have them anymore"); incandescent lightbulbs ("the Department of Energy has just banned them. They looked too good. So now you're stuck with some glowy fluorescent crap"); plastic straws; and laundry detergent.

"In Massachusetts now you can't throw out your old jeans and your old socks anymore. It's a civil offense to dispose of textiles. It makes you want to go throw T-shirts all over Martha's Vineyard just to break the law," he raged. "None of this is in your purview as a politician. Fix the freaking roads. You're totally incompetent. This is a country that was founded because people didn't want to pay a tea tax, and so they started a war."

Watching at home, I found it thrilling. Carlson is often passionate, but I'd never seen him this hot-blooded on TV perhaps ever. Which, in real time, even Carlson himself seemed to realize. He ended the segment by taking a breath and saying, not at all sheepishly, "I lost control, and I won't apologize for that."

Indeed, for most TV personalities, especially in the hothouse of cable news, such a display *would* be largely performance. But Carlson is one of the few who actually tones down on camera.

For even regular viewers, the tirade was as clear a look at the off-screen version of the man as they would see.

"My whole younger life was overshadowed by drinking too much," Tucker says, "and the fact is you don't experience things as deeply when you're drinking. You just miss a lot."

He was thirty-three years old when he got sober. It was a Saturday morning in August, 2002. His wife was twelve days away from giving birth to their fourth child, and he was fantastically hungover, he says, and seated at his desk, when something spoke to him. "It was almost like the pure word from God: If you keep doing that, you will destroy yourself and everything you love. I just had that dead-certain revelation, out of nowhere, and I just knew it was sure. It wasn't a question and I was like, 'Wow, Wow.' And I never had another drink. And it was super, super, super unpleasant, physically, to quit drinking."

Though Carlson was a highly functional alcoholic, his problem was utilitarian. "People who don't know anything about it, who haven't lived it, are always telling you that drinking is a crutch and you're using it for this or that," he says. "That's all true. But there's also the much more pressing concern of feeling like shit all the time. That's an actual concern, because you become physically dependent on alcohol. You use it to feel better. I'm speaking for myself, but everyone else I know says the same thing, the problem is you don't want to feel terrible."

His go-to was double screwdrivers; four shots of vodka at breakfast just to feel better and start the day. Because "drinking definitely does solve your problems, short term. You go from feeling so awful, like your whole soul is going to fly apart because of centrifugal force, a spinning inside like you're on a tilt-a-whirl, to feeling, like, really great. It really solves the problem immediately.

"So like any habit that's that powerfully reinforced it's going to be a really tough habit to break. And the physical dependency – I mean, I think the number is half of all chronic alcoholics who quit drinking, if untreated, die from the withdrawal. The same is true with Benzos. Benzodiazepines. That's not true of heroin. It's not true of cocaine. It's not true of meth, but Benzos and alcohol have enormously high death rates, multiples of Covid, higher than smallpox. People die from withdrawal."

Carlson says it took four months before his hands stopped shaking. "I felt like I had Parkinson's. It was intense, super intense. And then I just felt so much better. It was crazy how much better I felt."

The experience has left Tucker with profound sympathy for others in the grip of addiction and, indeed, for human frailty itself. "You know," he tells me, when the subject next arises, "Hunter Biden and I talked many, many times about sobriety."

"Really?"

He seems surprised by my surprise. "I knew him well, he was a friend and a neighbor of ours in D.C.," he explains, though his tone makes clear that on this subject he sets aside judgment on both ideological difference and behavioral excess. "He and his wife and kids came and stayed with us in Maine. Our wives were very close, they

TUCKER'S FOREBEARS: Great, great grandfather Henry Miller, California's "Cattle King"

Miller's daughter Ernestine McNear Carpenter as a child, circa 1898

Ernestine again, in a 1962 society page item, with granddaughter Lisa Lombardi, Tucker's mother.

Coming ... Museum West!

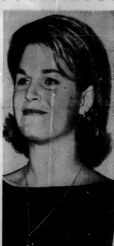

Grandmother, Mrs. Lewis Carpenter (left), and granddaughter, Lisa Lombardi, met William Barrett, president of the American Craftsman's Council at cocktails Friday

Tucker and
Buckley
Carlson...

...1975

... 2009

The Carlsons, soon after Lisa left the family

Dick and Tucker treasure hunting in La Jolla

Employee/friend Fred Takasawa and wedding guests

Dick on assignment for KFMB-TV, San Diego

"My father embodies everything I associated with journalism. He was smart, curious, relentlessly skeptical."

Dropouts Tucker and Susie stage their own "graduation"

LITERARY HEROES

Hunter S.
Thompson

P.J.
O'Rourke

With best friend
and Daily Caller
co-founder
Neil Patel…

…and improbable friend, James Carville

In the Maine
woods with
Brookie

Susie never
watched
the show,
but
critiqued
every
monologue

"Look at those beer girls. Can you believe they have legs like that?"

With executive producer Justin Wells

"Retirement is going great so far!"

were running partners. I loved Hunter's wife, Kathleen, I thought she was so impressive.

"Kathleen was always setting aside her own interests and duties to be the dutiful daughter-in-law. Jill Biden — excuse me, *Dr.* Jill — was a nasty person. Famously small-minded and dumb. If Dr. Jill didn't want to go on foreign trips, Kathleen would go, just to be a good daughter-in-law. The family was very clannish that way, which I admired. I like clannishness. They would think as a group.

"But they certainly weren't liberal, I'll tell you that. Hunter Biden was not liberal in any sense that I recognized. Biden has since become a trans activist and all that, but his family, they were pretty darn Catholic. They weren't anti-gun at all. Hunter and Kathleen weren't for abortion. They're the old Democratic party, the white working-class Democratic party, that does not exist anymore. Biden was about the last relic of that.

"Not that there was ever much depth to Joe Biden. He was famously stupid. Everyone always said he was stupid, and that he'd say anything. So that hasn't changed — he was always skin-deep, fake, and shallow, with the hair plugs, and face lifts, and the pat-you-on-the-back stuff. But he was always very friendly.

"Hunter, though, always struggled with this drug thing, and it really started to fall apart when he got busted and thrown out of the Navy for testing positive for cocaine. That was the beginning of the end.

"There are two categories of alcoholics, the ones who are so grateful every day to feel good, and those who always want to go back. He was one of those guys always one cocktail away from a bender. I've known many people like that. It's purely self-destructive, it really is like being completely possessed by demons. Look at Hunter, no matter what you now think of him or the family as public figures, the guy really hurt his daughters and his wonderful wife, totally wrecked her life, humiliated his father, whom he really loves. That's real. And his dad really loves him. He hurt all these people, hurt himself, degraded himself. Why would you take pictures of yourself with no teeth? Or take pictures of yourself with M&Ms on your dick? Take yourself pictures of yourself smoking crack or getting a hand job? But that's what you do, you just destroy things, you destroy people, even though it's super obvious there's no upside."

CHAPTER
TEN

B y the turn of the new century, Carlson was a contributor to a host of mainstream publications and fast becoming a regular face on TV. Three weeks after the September 11, 2001 attacks, with a red-hot America set to intervene in the region, *New York* magazine — which had just named him the journalist "Most Likely to Succeed in the Bush Years" — sent him to Pakistan, from where he planned to cross into Afghanistan. Even for a veteran adventure seeker it was a dangerous assignment, and it nearly cost him his life, though not in the way he expected. Before he even made it into Afghanistan, he had to head back to the States to appear on CNN's *Crossfire*, and as his plane flew over the Arabian Sea en route to Dubai, there was a terrific noise as something ripped off the undercarriage. Shaking violently, the plane dropped, then continued flying sideways, before finally skidding onto the runway, bouncing into a sand dune, coming to rest on its side, and catching fire. It should have exploded into a fireball, but somehow it didn't.

In 2003, Carlson was nominated for a National Magazine Award for an *Esquire* piece about traveling to Africa with Al Sharpton.

Sharpton's stated goal was to negotiate a peace among the rival factions in war-torn Liberia, and among the others accompanying him on the quixotic quest were the academic Cornel West and assorted other black activists. Disorganization and chaos reigned throughout, and in parts Carlson's account is hilarious. On the Air Ghana flight over, some in the party rage against the in-flight entertainment: a vintage *I Love Lucy* episode, with the sound coming over the PA system. With their plans changing moment to moment, the peacemakers never even make it to Liberia, while Tucker himself ends up hanging around with a pair of black Muslims, both named James Muhammad. "From their point of view, I was an irredeemable White Devil, cursed by Allah and marked for destruction," but the three get along famously, and the Muhammads affectionately dubbed him Tucker X.

Yet along the way, Carlson also found there was more to the notorious Reverend Sharpton than he'd expected. "We talked for hours over the course of the week, about everything from marriage to the Iowa caucuses," he wrote. "By the end, I'd settled at least one question: Sharpton doesn't hate whites after all. He just hates white liberals.

"You've dealt with inoffensive Negroes," Sharpton roared, imagining that he was talking to Terry McAuliffe or some other Democratic-party official. "Now you've got to deal with Al Sharpton." Sharpton knows that many white Democrats are embarrassed that he exists. The street-hustler wardrobe, Tawana Brawley, the hair — he is a public-relations disaster for the Democratic party, a living explanation of why suburbanites vote Republican. The thought fills him with pleasure, because it means that he has the power to make white Democrats uncomfortable every time he speaks. . . . "The only people who don't respect me are white liberals," he said one night at dinner. Some have dismissed him outright as a buffoon (he became furious just thinking about it); others have merely patted him on the head and tried to send him on his way. That's how it felt, anyway. He saw it happen to Jesse Jackson, who started out as an independent man of the left and wound up a party hack, summoned to the Clinton White House periodically like a servant to perform . . .

It is a measure of the lamentable state of today's journalism that in pretty much every print or online piece that pretends an interest in Carlson's origin story, this sharply observed and carefully considered piece of reporting is taken to be racist.

Later in 2003, *Esquire* sent him to Iraq.

Already thirteen journalists had died in Iraq that year, and before embarking on the trip, Carlson wrote letters to his wife and kids and composed a will. Arriving, he found flights into Baghdad had just been suspended following a string of surface-to-air missile strikes on commercial planes.

He'd later write in his book *The Long Slide* that the Iraq trip changed his views more profoundly than anything else he ever wrote. "I arrived a tepid supporter of the war, and of neoconservatism more generally. I returned home a determined opponent of both. The reality of Iraq bore no resemblance to the debates we were having back in Washington. The occupation was so clearly a disaster, even early on."

Entitled "Hired Guns: Inside the Not-So-Secret Armies of Operation Iraqi Freedom," the piece described Carlson's experience embedded with civilian contractors, among them heavily armed ex-Marines with whom he crossed the border from Kuwait. One night, the compound where he was staying came under attack by gunfire. It was a jittery, gloomy week in Baghdad's Green Zone, where he stayed— a marooned outpost of huddled interlopers engulfed in shapeless, ethereal peril, reminiscent of Joseph Conrad's *Heart of Darkness* or J.M. Coetzee's *Waiting for the Barbarians.* No one was ever quite sure where the threat came from, or who was shooting at them — Al Qaeda, Baath Party disciples, cartels of random street criminals, or even trigger-happy, improperly vetted fellow Western contractors.

The experience precipitated Carlson's first, notable public break from Beltway conservatism; and it permanently revised his thinking about the limits of American power and, even more so, the titanic risks of overreach.

"The Americans occupying Iraq couldn't even admit to themselves they were colonialists," he later wrote. "Instead, the State Department dressed up the whole operation like it was a kind of armed sensitivity training seminar, designed to liberate Iraqi women from their traditional gender roles. ... The result was failure, accompanied by chaos on every level. Watching it, I realized that there was nothing conservative about neoconservatism. The neocons were just liberals with guns, the most destructive kind."

Nearly two decades later, opposition to ill-considered American interventionism would be a staple on his primetime Fox show — one that following Russia's February 2022 invasion of Ukraine, would bring down on him new levels of character assassination. As the singular voice in cable news pointedly questioning America's growing involvement in the conflict, he found himself at odds with not just much of the Fox News lineup, but also with the editorial (and often the news) pages of other Murdoch properties like *The Wall Street Journal* and especially the *New York Post,* which daily featured a Ukrainian flag on its front page masthead. The rising tension with his fellow Fox primetime star Sean Hannity soon became apparent to even casual viewers when the two anchors ceased the brief chummy chat that had accompanied the handoff from one's program to the other's.

On his show, Carlson taunted and castigated with mounting vehemence pro-war senators such as Lindsey Graham, a once-frequent guest who now refused to appear on his show, before materializing the next hour for a softball turn with Hannity aimed at selling Republican voters on increased funding for the war effort.

"The uniparty is alive and well despite the best efforts of voters . . ." Carlson told his audience, with undisguised scorn, in December 2022. "And if you doubt that it's alive and well, here's a picture of Zelenskyy that he had taken with a group of elderly Republican senators in Kiev back in May. They stand grinning next to him in their orthopedic shoes. Seventy-year-old Susan Collins, John Barrasso, John Cornyn, led by their eighty-year-old ringleader, Mitch McConnell. Forty-four-year-old Zelenskyy poses between them in a skintight polo shirt, flexing like a weightlifter and trying to look ferocious. They seem awestruck. Not since a young Fidel Castro showed up in New York wearing battle fatigues has this country's aging leadership class tittered more loudly in delight. They love a man in uniform. What a hunk. So strong and decisive. Look at the expression on Mitch McConnell's face, you could almost hear the giggles of pleasure."

It was a dangerous stance to take, but Carlson stepped into the minefield without hesitation.

It would later be widely speculated that his stance on Ukraine was a major factor in Fox's taking him off the air. Carlson himself is unsure — the network gave him no explanation — but he certainly doesn't discount the possibility.

CHAPTER
ELEVEN

I f O.J. Simpson hadn't murdered his wife, I probably wouldn't be working in television," wrote Carlson in his 2003 memoir *Politicians, Partisans, and Parasites: My Adventures in Cable News,* published when he was thirty-four. "After years of writing political stories for newspapers and magazines, I thought I knew all about hostile responses from the public. Then I went into television. For pure red-in-the-face, neck-bulging, I-know-where-you-live-buddy reactions, nothing beats TV. It brings out the crazy in people."

As he tells it, one day in the fall of 1995 he happened to come back from lunch early, take-out hot dog in hand, and a receptionist at *The Weekly Standard,* where he worked at the time, asked what he knew about the O.J. trial. Dan Rather's booker had called looking for someone to appear on CBS's *48 Hours* to discuss the case. Carlson admits he knew relatively little about the case, but anyone who might know more was still at lunch. So by the end of the day he was on his way to New York for his first television appearance.

As he observes, people spend years training to be doctors or lawyers, but he became a TV talking head in about twelve hours.

"The whole experience had raised troubling questions about the way the world works: What did I know about the Simpson case that the rest of the population didn't? Was I really the most qualified person to explain the effect of the trial on American society? If not, why was I pretending to be? And why was a major news network allowing me to do it?" he asked. "I realized later that I had been applying print standards to television. But print isn't television. Both are forms of journalism, just as jogging and roller skating are both forms of forward motion. They're not the same. They require different skills. They operate by different rules."

Though he never again discussed the Simpson case on television, Carlson was now in the talking head club. "It wasn't that my one appearance had been a smashing success. The important thing was that it had happened. The world of talk show guests is like a closed union: You can't join unless you're already a member. Bookers resist booking people they've never seen on television. Conversely, once you've been booked, you're bookable. The process is self-authenticating."

Still, his television career was nearly derailed before it got seriously started by a mentally ill stalker. The deranged fan — an Indiana woman named Kimberly Carter, who wrote him letters referring to herself as his biggest fan and sent him a keychain and ballpoint pen as gifts — claimed she overheard a friend say Carlson would be at a pizza joint in Louisville, Kentucky, and, by her account, he either slipped narcotics into her drink or knocked her unconscious at the restaurant and violently raped her, presumably in front of dozens of patrons and staff. Carlson had never been to Louisville, let alone heard of the restaurant, and was most likely live on-air in a

Washington, D.C. television studio at time of the alleged incident, and of course no charges were ever filed.

Nonetheless, the world being what it is, he ended up having to spend close to $14,000 in legal fees to deal with the charge and the small-town "weasel" of an attorney the woman had gotten to pursue it.

"I knew the network would fire me immediately if it found out about the [attorney's accusatory] letter, and certainly if charges were filed against me," Carlson wrote afterward. "The one thing every journalist knows for certain about sex scandals is that they're always true. Partly true anyway. Maybe you didn't rape this woman, they'd think; maybe you just had unusually rough sadomasochistic sex with her and she misconstrued it. Or maybe your affair with her simply fell apart in an acrimonious way, perhaps over your cocaine habit. Maybe you had sex with her but never knew her name. Something definitely happened between you, though. People don't just make up specific allegations out of nothing."

The woman later apologized and retracted the claim, admitting "I was delusional," and suffered from schizoaffective disorder. (She would later attempt to rekindle a correspondence with Carlson, even wishing him a happy birthday).

Five years after the O.J. trial, Carlson got a call asking if he'd like to host a new show on CNN. It was a month before the 2000 election, and the show was meant to provide commentary and analysis after each of the coming debates, conservative Tucker paired with liberal Bill Press. Since it was more or less modeled on the rapid-response press operations set up by the campaigns, with each side trying to win the public-relations war, it was to be called "The Spin Room."

The broadcasts enjoyed modest success, and, following the election, *The Spin Room* became a real show, filling the late-night slot previously devoted mainly to broadcast reruns.

Basically, CNN executives treated *The Spin Room* as an afterthought, so much so that all these years later, the show doesn't even have a Wikipedia page. Carlson and Press were left to do mostly anything they wanted on air, including furnishing their own set, which they did through viewer donations. Taking note of the original barren set, which only included two chairs, a coffee table, and for backdrop a television on a rolling metal stand, it started when one viewer mailed the show a throw rug woven with the Wyoming state flag. Carlson and Press lavishly thanked the viewer on air and asked for more gifts, which led to a tidal wave of stuff arriving in the mail at the CNN office, from CDs, paintings, taxidermy, board games, and self-published manuscripts, to every sort of imaginable knick-knack and doodad. There was also plenty of food — which the hosts sometimes ate on air, something usually seen as a major TV faux pas. They eventually set aside an entire block each night featuring viewer benefactions and pleading for more.

Among the items that showed up in particular profusion were bow ties, with which Tucker was already becoming identified.

For all the passion of *The Spin Room*'s band of devoted fans, the show was roundly panned by critics.

"Press is a hopeless, dithering wimp who makes Carlson's bow-tied twit look like The Rock," declared *Entertainment Weekly* in 2001. "Between them, Carlson and Press would be hard-pressed to win a debate with network weatherman Flip Spiceland over whether or not the sun is out in Atlanta." *Salon* called it "the worst show in the history of CNN," while others raked the show as "amateurish," "sophomoric," "lightweight," and a "small-market talk radio show."

Impressed by the sheer furor of the denunciations, Carlson and Press half-seriously lobbied the network to use the line "the worst show in the history of CNN," in an ad campaign. The promotions department was less than charmed by the notion.

That the network was concerned about hostile press spoke to Tucker's growing realization of the distinctions between television and print journalism. "When you work in print," he wrote in 2001, as a television newbie, "a hostile response to your work is considered a sign that you may be doing something right. Of course they're upset, goes the reasoning; people always get mad when you tell the truth. It's a rare magazine writer who gets fired for eliciting nasty letters to the editor. I used to take pride in my hate mail. People don't think like that in television. Television is a purely democratic medium. Success has one measure: the number of people who watch."

Astonishingly, CNN's promotions department gave them the runaround even about getting official *Spin Room* coffee mugs for the hosts to use on the air. Carlson and Press had already asked viewers to send in design ideas, which they featured on the show, but CNN refused to invest the four dollars. After eight months of misdirection, Carlson woke up one morning determined to get it done and phoned someone in CNN's PR office. Haltingly, she put him off, suggesting he call the CNN gift shop in Atlanta.

He'd soon learn what he should have known at that moment — her reaction had nothing to do with coffee mugs.

Long before, after all, his father had told him of how, when he worked for ABC in Los Angeles, every year the station would pay for new suits to wear on air — until one year the suits didn't arrive. So Dick called the tailor. "There are no suits," the tailor told him, which is how he learned he'd been fired.

That evening, Carlson and Press had dinner with their boss, and were told *The Spin Room* had been canceled.

Tucker writes that as a kid, he used to wonder: "What sort of weird business is it where the guy who makes your clothes knows more about your future than you do? Twenty-five years later, I finally understood. Sooner or later, just about everyone in television gets canned, usually without warning."

In fact, among the many curiosities about Tucker's later cancellation by Fox, is that it occurred on a Monday. More typically, *The Spin Room* got axed on a Friday, with no on-air bon voyage or even an announcement to viewers. By 10:30 the following Monday night, it was as if the whole thing had never happened.

"It's best not to link your sense of self too closely to the success of whatever show you happen to be working on," Tucker observes presciently. "It could all end tomorrow, and likely will."

Still under contract to CNN, both Carlson and Press were moved over to *Crossfire*, CNN's longest-running political show. The program pitted liberal pundits against their conservative counterparts to discuss current affairs, and Carlson was to rotate with Bob Novak on the conservative side, replacing the show's prior lone conservative host, Mary Matalin, wife of James Carville, who was leaving to work in the Bush White House; Press joined as one of the liberal cohosts, but would last less than a year.

After Press was fired, *Crossfire*, originally launched in 1982, underwent a dramatic revamp, moving from a studio at CNN's Washington, D.C., bureau to a 250-seat auditorium at George Washington University, with Carville and Paul Begala brought in as the new liberal cohosts.

Shortly before the revamped version was to debut, CNN's Washington bureau chief Frank Sesno pulled Carlson into his office. "You're about to break out," he told him. "People are going to start to recognize you. Don't let it go to your head. Don't become an asshole."

The advice was unnecessary. "If anything," wrote Carlson in 2003, "the new attention made me feel less confident. Within days of the first show, people whose opinions I had never sought called me to critique my performance on the air. A magazine editor cornered me at a cocktail party in New York and spent twenty minutes explaining how the camera angles on *Spin Room* made me look freakish, like an ugly man in a funhouse mirror. Right away I learned that television brings out the critic in almost everyone. ... And, of course, sometimes they're right, which is why it's so painful. Hardest of all to get used to, though, was the loss of anonymity in public. Working in television is like having your picture in the post office. People you've never seen before know what you look like."

Given the personalities involved, all deeply committed philo-sophically and skilled at verbal thrust and parry, the new *Crossfire* soon became blood sport. It was shortly after the disputed 2000 election, and for the aggrieved Left, the brief embrace of patriotism after 9/11 soon gave way, with the Iraq War, to new levels of outrage, with Bush cast as (the pre-Trump) Hitler. On the show passions ran high and tempers often flared. Each night the hosts, both left and right, brought on a guest to help argue their side, and as always, nothing was surer to arouse Tucker Carlson's indignation than a party-line hack, mindlessly regurgitating the official line.

"Being a blind partisan defeats the whole purpose of being an adult," he wrote at the time. "Once you grow up, you're meant to develop your own grown-up opinions about things. You're supposed to disregard what Mommy says and say what you really think. Some people can't handle this. They want to be bossed around and told what to believe. They want to take orders. They're only comfortable expressing preapproved thoughts. Reflexive party loyalty was made for people who miss Mommy's firm hand."

On the other hand, he always had a soft spot for those with strong and unshakeable beliefs, regardless of the creed. "No matter how crackpot the opinion, I can respect a deeply held view. I may not believe the earth is flat, but if you sincerely do, I won't hate you for it. We've had a lot of true believers on *Crossfire*. I don't think I've ever yelled at one."

He says that when he did lose his cool and get personal in his attacks, he always regretted it afterward. "Getting personal is probably more offensive to a lot of people (including me) than swearing. I hate doing it."

A second important piece of advice about being on television had come from Larry King. At the 2000 Democratic Convention in Los Angeles, the venerable TV host pulled Tucker aside out of nowhere. "Let me tell you something about this business," he said. "The trick is to care, but not too much. Give a shit — but not really." Calling it "King's Law of Detachment," Carlson used those words as an epigram in his first book and has lived by them since, "mostly out of an instinct for self-preservation," he says.

King wasn't talking about being disingenuous on air. He meant not getting too wrapped up in the hype, not believing your own bullshit. Every job in television is a temp job. Everyone is replaceable and will be replaced, as swiftly as they appeared. To become too emotionally or psychologically invested in your position is to court catastrophe.

It was a lesson that would serve Carlson well over the years, and of course more than ever when the highest ratings in the business failed to prevent his being blindsided by Fox.

One thing Carlson had no need to learn was candor. That has always come naturally, and even as a far more traditional conservative than the iconoclast he would become — which is to say, far more trusting of the powers that be — he held the same views on the air as off.

Not that that won him any points with liberals, who've often assumed that even the brightest and most charismatic of their ideological adversaries — think William F. Buckley — had to be insincere. As Carlson has continuously observed, being unable to fathom anyone but halfwits holding views other than their own, liberals dismiss conservatives by definition as grifters, opportunists, attention-seekers, and chaos agents without principle or genuine conviction.

In this regard, Carlson well knows that not only is he no exception, but has lately been regarded as the reigning number-one example of right-wing ethical/intellectual fraud.

At the time he was known, and frequently mocked, for his bow ties, though he'd been sporting them his entire adult life. "My dad wore one, so I started wearing one in ninth grade," he tells me. "I lived in such a tiny world — I guess we all do — I didn't realize how freakish it was." He finally gave it up in 2006 when someone at a public event told him it was a good "branding device." "The implication was that it was false," he recalls, "like it was something my agent had told me to wear to stand out. I was so horrified by the idea that it was seen as a branding device that I immediately gave it up and I've never worn one again."

Even at the time there was a band of lefty journalists keeping a close eye on Carlson for transgressions that could potentially be useful in ideological warfare. But over time, with his rising stature, and the enormous success of *Tucker Carlson Tonight*, they grew into a veritable sub-industry of writers, podcasters, Media Matters–style apparatchiks, monitoring his every public (and even private) word in search of ammunition to dismiss the whole thing as an (exceedingly dangerous) act.

Tellingly, one media leftist, Democratic Socialist Carlos Maza, writing in Vox, actually turned to Marx to explain Carlson's otherwise inexplicable appeal, asserting he had tricked the white working class "into accepting its own exploitation. By focusing his audience's attention on insignificant culture war stories, Carlson is able to create a fictional version of 'the elite' — vegans, anti-racist activists, feminists, etc. — while distracting from the political party that actually holds the power in government. Carlson's faux-populism is an act."

"If you're a Democrat," declared Media Matters's Katherine Abughazaleh, (whose "full immersion" online coverage of Tucker-

World provided "the valuable service of watching Tucker so liberals don't have to,") "you should not be going on Tucker Carlson's show."

"I'm always amazed by how many people assume that talk show hosts are merely pretending to be outraged or interested in the things they talk about," Tucker wrote in *Politicians, Partisans, and Parasites*. "I set them straight right away. Actually, I say, I believe every bit of it, sometimes more than I say on the air. They hate hearing this, but it's true. In fact, I do believe everything I say. You have to. Arguing a position you don't really support is a sure way to wind up loathing yourself. Plus, genuine conviction makes for a good debate. Phoniness is easy to spot. Which is not to say I don't have occasional doubts. There are plenty of issues I don't have strong feelings about. There are plenty more that are easier to defend in the abstract than in real life."

Still, for all *Crossfire*'s occasional pyrotechnics, America was a very different place in those years, with political differences far less likely to threaten personal relationships, and even bitter ideological rivals were usually able to keep things at least somewhat in perspective. In one classic 2003 clip from the show, a month after the release of Hillary Clinton's memoir *Living History*, Carlson leaps in surprise when Hillary suddenly walks onto the set. For months, Tucker has told viewers he would eat his shoe if the book sold a million copies, and publisher Simon & Schuster having announced the book reached that milestone, a grinning Hillary, in teal pantsuit, carries a cake in the shape of a shoe.

"Hello, Tucker," she says. "I want you to know, Tucker, this is a wingtip. It's a *right*-wing tip." she added. As the audience breaks up, a beaming Tucker shakes her hand.

Obviously, in today's climate it is impossible to imagine any such scene on a cable news broadcast today, right or left.

Indeed, Tucker mentioned in 2023 on the podcast *Full Send* that all these years later he still has "one friend who's a personality at CNN," but "I can't say this person's name because it'll wreck this person's career."

(Laughingly, he added that CNN star Don Lemon — who in a freak media concurrence a week later would lose his job the same day as Tucker — though "the stupidest person who's ever had a TV show, and that's saying a lot," had "massive flair" and otherwise seemed like "a good dude.")

Over its life, *Crossfire* would expose Carlson to a rogues' gallery of political types across the ideological spectrum, many of whom would still be key players when Carlson came to rule the cable airwaves on Fox. For instance, one of the most frequent guests on *Crossfire* was Mike Pence, and for Carlson, Pence was, even as a young, obscure Indiana congressman, "creepy as hell. There's something strange about Pence. I've been around him a lot, and always felt that he was a totally sinister figure, craven and dishonest.

"I don't think the Pence you see is the real Pence. I just get a very, very strange vibe off that guy — he makes me extremely uncomfortable. Everything about Pence is false. I don't know why nobody says that. If you are talking to someone who seems false on every level, then the obvious question is, 'What is he hiding?'" Carlson says.

Carlson would bear this very much in mind during the early days of Covid, when Donald Trump tapped Vice President Pence to oversee the response to the looming pandemic. "Trump put everything in Pence's hands, and my feeling — I can't prove it — was that from day one Pence was there to undermine Trump and to keep an eye on him. I know that Trump doesn't seem to think this, he seems to kind of like Pence. But I always felt Pence was getting all his instructions from Fauci, and he was pushing Trump in the wrong direction. That doesn't absolve Trump from hiring Fauci or locking down the country. Trump was president; he's responsible for that. But I do think Pence played a big role in how it played out."

While at CNN, Carlson also briefly hosted a primetime weekly public-affairs program on PBS called *Tucker Carlson: Unfiltered.*

At the time the publicly funded network was coming under increasing scrutiny for its left-wing tilt, and many took Carlson's hiring as a defensive move. "I've heard that before," Tucker acknowledged at the time, adding that his aim was simply to put on good television. "The standards are going to be pretty clear: tell me something I don't know, and no lying. They're simple, but you rarely see that on TV, so it's harder than it sounds."

Nearly twenty years later, no longer embarrassed by its institutional leftist bias — indeed, flaunting it — PBS felt it necessary to justify having once hired "the high priest of Trumpism," as one network guest termed him. PBS's signature news program *Newshour* ran an entire segment purporting to show how, since his long-ago stint, Carlson's views had become "increasingly extreme." "We should remind folks," noted PBS's Amna Nawaz, "he's had a long history, a long career in television. He's been through multiple networks. He had shows at MSNBC and CNN, right here on PBS, a short-lived show as well. He was offering sort of a conservative, libertarian point of view."

Today, though, a guest on the segment pointed out, Carlson is responsible for "the most racist show in history. . . . Every night, that show teaches fear and loathing. He may claim to be a person who opposes racism and prejudice, but what the show tells you every night is to be afraid, to be afraid of people who are in the street asking for police officers to not shoot black people."

Still, before joining the Fox News primetime lineup, it is from *Crossfire* that Tucker was known — and, for many, only from the single infamous episode that would prove to be its death knell.

That broadcast was on October 15, 2004, and featured an appearance by the popular liberal comedian and *Daily Show* host, Jon Stewart. He was supposedly on *Crossfire* to promote his new book, *America (The Book)*, but instead used his allotted time to eviscerate the show and its hosts.

"I made a special effort to come on the show today," he announced, sitting between the blindsided hosts, "because I have privately, amongst my friends and also in occasional newspapers and television shows, mentioned this show as being bad. I felt that that wasn't fair and I should come here and tell you that I don't — it's not so much that it's bad, as it's hurting America."

Of their treatment of politicians, he added: "You're not too rough on them. You're part of their strategies. You are partisan, what do you call it, hacks. You're doing theater when you should be doing debate. What you do is not honest. What you do is partisan hackery."

For all his startling moral high-handedness, the highly partisan Stewart's own hands were hardly clean in this regard.

"I think you're a good comedian," responded Carlson, but "I think your lectures are boring. You had John Kerry on your show and you sniff his throne and you're accusing *us* of partisan hackery?"

In fact, he'd had the Democratic presidential nominee (who'd refused to face tough questioning on *Crossfire*) on *The Daily Show* just weeks before and fed him nothing but softballs.

"I'm just saying," pressed Carlson, "there's no reason for you — when you have this marvelous opportunity not to be the guy's butt boy, to go ahead and be his butt boy. Come on. It's embarrassing."

"I was absolutely his butt boy," agreed Stewart with an impish smile, dodging the point. "I was so far — you would not believe what he ate two weeks ago."

Then, not missing a beat, he was back on the attack. "You know, you have a responsibility to the public discourse, and you fail miserably."

"You need to get a job at a journalism school, I think," Carlson shot back. "I thought you were going to be funny. Come on. Be funny."

"No. I'm not going to be your monkey."

"Is this really Jon Stewart?" demanded Carlson. "What is this, anyway? What's it like to have dinner with you? It must be excruciating. Do you, like, lecture people like this or do you come over to their house and sit and lecture them; they're not doing the right thing, that they're missing their opportunities, evading their responsibilities?"

"If I think they are," Stewart fired back.

"I wouldn't want to eat with you, man. That's horrible," Carlson said.

"I know. And you won't," Stewart said.

"I do think you're more fun on your show. Just my opinion," Carlson said.

"You know what's interesting, though? You're as big a dick on your show as you are on any show," Stewart responded.

In fact, looking at it now, Carlson more than held his own.

He'd later call Stewart's appearance "lame and kind of sanctimonious," even while acknowledging some of what he said had merit. "The real criticism I believe is that that form of debate can be inauthentic [...] It's phony when people argue for a team."

Begala later wrote of being similarly blindsided by Stewart's behavior. "From my perspective, the show that day was a debacle. I was unprepared for the onslaught since Stewart had recently been on *Hannity & Colmes*," Begala wrote, referencing the Fox News show with a format not unlike *Crossfire*'s. "And he had not attacked that show at all. But he had a different agenda this day."

After the taping, Stewart, Carlson, Begala, and Stewart's executive producer continued chatting for ninety more minutes, a dialogue that was earnest and constructive. But of course the audience never heard that part, and the damage was done.

In the aftermath, Stewart was widely portrayed as a concerned and deeply patriotic truth-teller. No one reported that as he was leaving the studio that day, he turned to Carlson and Begala and remarked, "Imus came to Washington and bashed you guys, and he got like three hundred new stations. So I think this will work out for me."

It did. Stewart's book became a mega best-seller, and nearly twenty years later, he still reminisces about the career-defining stunt.

"I called Tucker Carlson a dick on national [*sic*] television," he tweeted in 2021, looking to boost his diminished public profile. "It's high time I apologize... . . . . to dicks. Never should have lumped you in with that terrible terrible [*sic*] person."

If Carlson is often accused by those on the other side of playing a dick on television, Stewart apparently has no hesitation being one in real life. "I have not spoken to Jon Stewart since that day," fellow leftist Begala revealed in 2015. "I ran into him in a hotel lobby once, and he darted away like he'd seen a ghost. When I had a book I wanted to plug on his show, he wouldn't take my call."

Several months after the Stewart fracas, *Crossfire* was canceled, ending its twenty-two-year run on the air. (*Crossfire* would be briefly rebooted in 2013 with former Obama hands Van Jones and Stephanie Cutter on the left, and Newt Gingrich and S.E. Cupp on the right, but the hosts had little chemistry, and the show was canceled after less than a year.)

Though the original *Crossfire* had already seen a ratings slump prior to the Stewart episode, the comedian's vaunted takedown was seen as the fatal blow. CNN president Jonathan Klein all but confirmed this, telling *The New York Times* in 2005, "I agree wholeheartedly with Jon Stewart's overall premise," asserting he wanted to see the network move away from "head-butting debate shows." Begala remained with the network while Carlson departed.

"[Tucker Carlson's] career aspirations and our programming needs just don't synch up," Klein told the *Associated Press*. "He wants to host his own night-time show, and we don't see that in the cards here."

In fact, Carlson was already in negotiations with MSNBC, CNN's top competitor, for a show of his own. *The Situation with Tucker Carlson* premiered on MSNBC in June 2005, later changing its name to *Tucker* when it moved from the 11:00 p.m. timeslot to 6:00 p.m. Though PBS offered to renew Carlson's contract, he declined in order to focus on the MSNBC show. He did, however, in 2006, make time to appear in season three of ABC's *Dancing with the Stars*. "I think if you sat back and tried to plan my career, you might not choose this," he allowed at the time to The *Washington Post*. "But my only criterion is the interest level. I want to lead an interesting life. I'm 37. I've got four kids. I have a steady job. I don't do things that I'm not good at very often. I'm psyched to get to do that."

If nothing else, the show displayed his capacity to laugh at himself. Proclaiming "I'll be more nervous dancing than I was in Beirut," he came out in one episode in a sapphire-blue ruffled silk shirt unbuttoned nearly to his navel to perform the cha-cha with professional dance partner Elena Grinenko who wore an orange, fringe bikini. The dance begins with Grineko approaching him from behind, ripping the bow tie from Tucker's neck, and tossing it on the ground.

"I love that you had so much fun," remarked the kindest of the judges. "What an awful mess," countered the designated jerk on the panel, to a round of boos from the audience. Carlson was the first contestant voted off that season.

In March 2008, MSNBC canceled *Tucker*. The show had struggled to attract viewers and by then the network was fast moving to the left, reimagining its editorial mission as the liberal counterpart to Fox News. "I'm not attacking it, but they didn't have a role for me," he told *The New York Times*. "It's just a different network than it was when I joined. Very different."

Despite its disappointing performance, the show served to begin the reworking of Tucker's image in crucial ways. Having dropped the bow tie he'd sported since boarding school, which had long served to mark its youthful wearer as a whip-smart but wiseass frat boy, Tucker found his expensive neckties lent him a new sense of gravitas.

Curiously enough, the failed show also introduced to the public the figure who would emerge as Tucker's opposite number on the left. His producer, Tucker says, literally plucked a tape sent by the agent of little-known progressive radio talk-show host Rachel Maddow "out of the slush pile." Recognizing her chops, they immediately booked her. "I'd just come from *Crossfire*," Carlson says, and hoping his new format would feature as much light as heat, Maddow seemed a worthy opponent. He didn't want a pushover, he tells me, but an equal. "It keeps you limber, in fighting form. I didn't want to do the schtick they usually do, get some retarded person on. Liberals always have some retarded Klan member on — 'What you're saying is wrong! It's just wrong!'" he imitates an outraged liberal host. "I always hated that. It really is just dishonorable if you think of yourself as a professional debater, you know what I mean, which I always did. It would be like if you were a boxer and you're fighting some drunk guy in an exhibition. So, I felt that was beneath me, degrading, I want someone who's really smart. She's not really smart. She's really clever. She isn't a deep intellectual or anything, but I'm not either, but she's a good debater and super nice. I always liked her.

"My main love for her always came from her toughness. She's legit tough. The only complaint I ever had about her is that she wouldn't, in the end, change her mind, whereas I would have, although not very often. I had a core belief in fairness. If you have a better point, it's okay to concede to it. But you could give her photographic evidence and she still wouldn't."

On air, the two seemed to have genuine chemistry and mutual respect. In one episode, discussing a video released by Osama bin Laden, Carlson described the 9/11 mastermind's rhetoric as being in sync with that of top Democrats. "This is the only time I've been actively mad at you, but I'm mad!" came back Maddow. Yet even as she said it, seated alongside Carlson, she couldn't help laughing, clearly less angry than bemused by his brazen, over-the-top insolence.

Carlson smiled back. "When you spend the weekend meditating on this, I know you're going to come around."

In another episode — the topic was provocative comments made by conservative flamethrower Ann Coulter about September 11 widows — Carlson challenged Maddow's worldview (and liberalism's overall sense of its own moral superiority) in earnest. "[What] I have noticed over the years," he said, "is the liberal belief — and it's an article of faith — that suffering confers wisdom and, in fact, suffering does not confer wisdom. Because you have suffered through something — you have been the victim of this, that, or the other thing — does not mean you have moral authority that exceeds anyone else's moral authority. Nor does it mean you have particular insight or wisdom into anything."

"I don't think it's that victim equals expert," Maddow answered, equally serious. "I think what liberals — in particular academic liberals — have prioritized is people who have been there, people who have seen things firsthand, should be allowed to speak for their own experience. And whether that means you're a victim or whether that means you're an expert because you saw it with your own eyes, it's an eye-witnessed priority."

"How much does the left — I mean, it's like a seething obsession, right — hate Ann Coulter? I imagine everyone from Air America radio gets together to, whatever, eat macrobiotic food and smoke pot, Ann Coulter is a topic of conversation."

"Correct," replied Maddow, with a smile, retreating back to the common ground of friendship based on a skewed take on the world. "After we smoke pot there's not much talking, there is a lot of sleeping and twitching."

With the show canceled, Maddow took over *Tucker's* 9:00 p.m. timeslot with her own show and became the face of the reimagined far-left cable channel. By 2022, *The Rachel Maddow Show* was the only one of the ten top-rated cable news programs not on Fox. With an average 3.3 million nightly viewers, *Tucker Carlson Tonight* ranked second, while Fox's *The Five* was number one. Maddow was fifth overall, taking in 2.3 million viewers nightly.

After he left MSNBC Tucker would catch her show and often be intrigued by what she was covering. "The thing I really liked most about her, which I tried to learn from and emulate, is that she was completely disconnected from the news cycle," says Tucker now. "Television gets their stories from newspapers — left or right, it doesn't matter.

"Her view — I've never heard her say this but it's very obvious in watching her story selection — is the lead story is what *I* think is most important, not *The New York Times*. *I* determine what the lead is.

"That's much easier for me to do because by definition I don't care what *The New York Times* says. But if you're Rachel Maddow, it's harder, because she's part of that same ecosystem, and people in that ecosystem will be embarrassed if you completely ignore all five stories above the fold in *The New York Times*. But her view was, no, *I* lead, you follow. She really was alpha in that way, totally willing and completely happy to determine what the most important thing was, even if it was stuff way outside, and not covered by everybody else. She finds something she thought was interesting. And then she would tell this long story, and I just thought that was wonderful. I didn't agree with it, but as someone who makes TV shows, it was clear she's doing something different, she's doing better. It's the kind of thing you have to be in the business to respect. But I really respect that a lot. Because it's hard. People say, 'Well, that's not the big story today.' No, the big story is what I say it is, and actually that's why I get paid. Why else are you paying me? To read a script? No, it's to make these decisions about the relative importance of stories.

"And she did that first, she did it before I did. And it was like, 'Oh, wow, this is a good thing to do.'

"Because in my world, once you get away from the monopoly on storytelling, that's a big deal.

"Other shows, how do they have no ability to create a hierarchy of importance? Because placement really, really matters, emphasis matters. It's not just what you say, it's in what order you say it. Chronology forms the basis of a story. You put it in a certain order for a reason. For a joke, the punchline comes at the end. The form is the essence.

"That's the one thing no one ever questions. They question: is this good or bad? They question the qualitative part of it — we're coming to different conclusions about the same story. *But is this story itself worth talking about?*

"I think Rachel Maddow really helped alternative media. She was a big force in traditional media, she's on the NBC cable channel, and she broke from the formula."

"It was so ambitious, creative, and fresh. And it's your own; you're doing your own thing. Above all, I respect people who do their own thing. I don't have to enjoy the flavor to respect the work. If your whole way of thinking is a pivot against one thing, you're still controlled by that one thing."

I've heard Maddow described by even conservatives who know her as "the Tucker of the left" — not about politics, but in her likability off camera. As staff, coworkers, and even some fans might tell you, few television stars are pleasant people in real life. But Maddow and Carlson are exceptions.

In fact, Maddow was the only liberal media personality to so much as respond to an interview request for this book, and though she declined, it was very politely. A search of her Twitter account, active since 2008, reveals that Rachel Maddow has never once tweeted about Tucker Carlson.

Carlson remained at MSNBC as a special correspondent until his contract expired later that year, before joining Fox News as a contributor.

"After stints at CNN and MSNBC, Tucker Carlson is getting his pundit passport stamped by the third cable news network (and the most popular of the three), the Fox News Channel," a twenty-three-year-old rookie media reporter named Brian Stelter wrote in *The New York Times* at the time.

Tucker's first appearance as a Fox employee was on *Fox & Friends Weekend*. It fell on May 16, 2009, on the Saturday morning he turned forty years old.

"This is the very first thing I'm doing in my forties other than shaving," he joked on air.

Contributors cycle in and out of cable news networks. Indeed, what looks like a glamorous job, and one certainly much coveted, is not always what it appears from the outside. It is a position that is fickle and conditional in the extreme, and not necessarily even an especially lucrative one. At Fox, salaries for regular contributors can run as high as half a million dollars — the upper rungs generally reserved for ex-Republican administration officials (John Bolton pulled in $569,423) — but can go as low as $30,000 a year. During her seven-year tenure as a Fox national security analyst, even K.T. McFarland earned a relatively modest $63,518 a year.

Of course, for some, like McFarland, a cable news contributorship is a side gig. But Tucker was now putting four children through private school, and he effectively found himself with only part-time employment.

But there was also this in the story by Stelter, the future hard-left CNN host who would come to be known to Carlson's Fox audience as "the Eunuch":

"Mr. Carlson will be a paid contributor for Fox, appearing on programs to talk politics. Might the former CNN and MSNBC talk show host become a host of his own program on Fox, too?"

CHAPTER
TWELVE

B ehind the scenes it was one of the darkest periods of Carlson's
life — his personal time in the wilderness.

"It was super depressing," he says. "You think, who wouldn't
love four months off? Some people say, *I don't know how I'd spend the
time*. I know exactly what I'd do. I'd build a treehouse. I'd do building
projects. Except I didn't have a job on the other end. I couldn't relax."

That summer Maine's lakes saw an outbreak of Eurasian water-
milfoil, a fast-growing invasive aquatic plant from Asia that can reach
thirty feet in length. It fills entire lakes killing off native fish, crusta-
ceans, and plants, rendering waterways useless for recreation.

"The year I got fired I spent four months in Maine not working,
just pulling milfoil," Carlson recalls. "But it wasn't that fun because I
couldn't relax. So, we started the *Daily Caller*, because I had nothing
else to do."

The idea came up over dinner with his old college roommate Neil Patel one evening at The Palm in Washington, D.C. Patel was working for Vice President Dick Cheney at the time, but the administration was winding down.

The *Huffington Post* had launched a couple of years before, and served as an inspiration, if not precisely a model. "It was amazing," Patel tells me, "they had as much online traffic as *The Washington Post*. And through *HuffPo*, Arianna Huffington, who before was this *Washington Times* columnist and wife of a failed Senate candidate, became this huge A-lister. She starts this thing and it just took off and I was shocked that no one on the right was taking advantage of the opportunity that the internet afforded to enter the media space. You don't have to buy printing presses or need kids on bikes to throw newspapers at houses. You just have to hire a few reporters and throw up a website and you can start a news company. Still, I didn't really like the idea because they're shitty businesses. But I mentioned it to Tucker, and he said we should do it. 'I can run the news side and you can run the business.'"

(As a side note: According to the brilliant, late conservative provocateur Andrew Breitbart, who worked for Arianna Huffington before she veered sharply leftward, she'd originally launched the *Huffington Post* to provide a platform for liberals to beclown themselves, one which, as they bandied about their lunatic ideas, would be a vehicle for the left to eat itself. If so, the extent to which that was successful or its founding marked the beginning of the end of the United States, or both, has yet to be determined.)

"We wanted to abide by traditional norms of reporting," says Patel. "This is not a blog; it's not a bunch of kids' opinions. We'll hire people and send them to events and have them interview people and report facts."

Deliberating over the name, they more or less knew what they wanted: one that would bring to mind the substance of a respected traditional newspaper. But, being on a tight budget, any masthead featuring words like *Post, Times,* or *Journal* was already either taken or would cost thousands of dollars to secure the URL.

The problem was solved in extraordinary fashion. On February 11, 2006, Patel happened to be with Dick Cheney on a ranch near Corpus Christi, Texas when the vice president took aim at a quail and shot his hunting partner, Harry Whittington, in the face. Patel phoned Cheney aide Mary Matalin to report the episode and devise a strategy on how to deal with the press. Because it was a hunting accident, Cheney's team decided it could be passed off as a local news story. They would alert a nearby outlet and allow the story to filter onto the wires that way, thereby ignoring the Washington press completely. The local newspaper happened to be named the *Corpus Christi Caller.*

"I remembered that *Caller* was sort of an old newspaper name, so we went with the *Daily Caller* because it was free," Patel says.

Securing initial funding was a struggle. Carlson and Patel spent a year in meetings with venture capitalists in Boston, Chicago, Los Angeles, New York, San Francisco, and Toronto, eventually finding two firms that offered a collective $3 million to fund the company. Ready to sign the paperwork, Patel read through the legal documents and felt queasy; he'd been a lawyer and "had somewhat more business skills than Tucker," for whom "business was the farthest thing from his mind." "I was like, holy shit, these guys can fire us. It seemed like a lot of career risk to start a new company and give someone you barely know complete control over it. Media is not like a tech platform that's just going to roll in revenues at a high rate, which is what they're looking for. And if they don't like the results, it's normal to fire the founders. We didn't want to get fired. Plus, they wanted to install all this bureaucracy and we knew we needed to be nimble. So, we didn't like the idea, and thought maybe we could find a private investor."

They didn't take the deal.

Fortunately, soon after a friend in Jackson, Wyoming, set up a lunch with Foster Friess — a prominent businessman, devout Christian, and Republican Party donor, and Carlson and Patel jumped on a flight west. Twenty minutes into the lunch, before they'd finished their salads, Friess, who was known for his disdain for bureaucracy in corporate America, offered Patel and Carlson $3.5 million. Friess had only two caveats: he wanted nothing to do with the running the company, not even a seat on the board; and the two had to go pheasant hunting with him once a year in Gettysburg, South Dakota.

"Ok, we can do that!" Patel instantly agreed.

It turned out that the hunt, which he'd started, was a sacred annual tradition for Friess, the thirty-odd invitees including old friends, celebrities, business guys, religious leaders, and politicians — all with prescribed rules, including speakers at mealtime. Friess died in 2021, but the hunt continues, funded by a foundation he left behind.

"It's an amazing event," says Patel. "People really open up in this weird format that Foster created. Tucker and I have been doing it for many years."

The site launched in 2010 and became profitable in its second year. Its primary mission was to inject more original reporting into online conservative news, which was dominated by opinion. With Carlson acting as editor-in-chief and Patel running the business side, the *Daily Caller* became one of the most popular online conservative news sources in the U.S., attracting between fifteen and twenty million visitors per month, as well as the only conservative outlet listed as one of Facebook's nine U.S. fact-checking operations. The content ranged from investigations, breaking news, and beat reporting, to sexy-girl tabloid-style clickbait. Stories about attractive female teachers caught sleeping with male students was an especially popular staple.

In 2012, a piece jointly bylined by Carlson and Vince Coglianese, today the *Daily Caller*'s editorial director and long a guest on *Tucker Carlson Tonight*, broke a major story — or what would have been one, had the legacy media been interested in news that cast Barack Obama in any but the most positive light. The two reporters had gotten their hands on 2007 footage of then-Senator Obama, at the time about to launch his campaign for the presidency, giving a shockingly racially charged speech at traditionally black Hampton University to an audience of black ministers.

"For nearly 40 minutes," wrote Carlson and Coglianese, "using an accent he almost never adopts in public, Obama describes a racist, zero-sum society, in which the white majority profits by exploiting black America. The mostly black audience shouts in agreement. The effect is closer to an Al Sharpton rally than a conventional campaign event."

They reported that Obama's focus was on the supposed disparity between the federal aid dispatched to New Orleans after Hurricane Katrina and that sent to Florida following Hurricane Andrew, as well as to New York City in the wake of the September 11 attacks,, thundering about "the people down in New Orleans they [whites] don't care about as much!" because white Americans don't see blacks as "part of the American family."

It was an appalling performance, grounded in a ghastly lie. In fact, the *Daily Caller* reporters pointed out, by "January of 2007, six months before Obama's Hampton speech, the federal government had sent at least $110 billion to areas damaged by Katrina, compared to the mere $20 billion the Bush administration pledged to New York City after Sept. 11." Moreover, "on May 25, 2007, just weeks before the speech, the Bush administration sent an additional $6.9 billion to Katrina-affected areas with no strings attached."

"As a sitting United States Senator, Obama must have been aware of this," wrote Carlson and Coglianese. "And yet he spent 36 minutes at the pulpit telling a mostly black audience that the U.S. government doesn't like them because they're black.

"As the speech continues, Obama makes repeated and all-but-explicit appeals to racial solidarity, referring to 'our' people and 'our' neighborhoods,' as distinct from the white majority."

What's startling, and of course should have been of immense interest to news consumers across the spectrum, is that at the time candidate Obama was at pains to nurture his "carefully-crafted image as a leader eager to build bridges between ethnic groups." Instead, "Obama, who was not using a teleprompter, deviated from his script repeatedly, ad-libbing lines that he does not appear to have used before any other audience during his presidential run.

"Most surprisingly, he offers a full-throated defense of Jeremiah Wright, the Chicago pastor in whose church he had sat for twenty years, and whose racially inflammatory and anti-American rants were by then already becoming a problem for the burgeoning campaign. Not only does Obama open the speech with 'a special shout out' to Wright, who was in the audience, but he goes on to defiantly characterize him as, 'my pastor, the guy who puts up with me, counsels me, listens to my wife complain about me. He's a friend and a great leader. Not just in Chicago, but all across the country.'"

Needless to say, in due course Obama would drop Wright like a bad habit, and condemn his vile views in no uncertain terms.

Yet what made Carlson and Coglianese's revelation so meaningful even five years later was less what it said about the media's happy service as Obama's Praetorian guard — by now that was old news — but what it revealed about the depths of Obama's own racism and his view of the country he led. For, by 2012, Obama's true views were doing grievous damage, both within his party and to the nation at large.

In this sense, the *Daily Caller* piece was both important and prescient.

Carlson and his co-author close their report by noting the small but vital differences between the way Obama's speech ended in the printed draft distributed to the media and the way he actually ended it.

The first reads: "America is going to survive. We won't forget where we came from. We won't forget what happened 19 months ago, 15 years ago, thousands of years ago."

The second: "America will survive. Just like black folks will survive. We won't forget where we came from. We won't forget what happened 19 months ago, or 15 years ago, or 300 years ago."

"Three hundred years ago," wrote Carlson and Coglianese. "It's a reference the audience understood."

The piece was characteristic of the *Daily Caller* brand — scrappy and determinedly *not* part of the herd. The outlet was not above noting that conservative icon Rush Limbaugh might have been "insensitive and intolerant," as in one piece Tucker editorialized he himself had been in his characterization of a feminist law-school student, even while making the more crucial point that the resulting advertising boycott of Limbaugh's show was farcical. "There's almost nothing that upsets Americans more than the idea that somewhere, somehow somebody is getting his feelings hurt," as he mockingly wrote. "In the eyes of most of us, that's a sin worse than murder. Literally."

Over the years, the *Daily Caller* has continued as not just an independent voice, but also one that regularly benefits from "exclusives" that no one else pursues simply by virtue of their subjects.

"The only reason the *Daily Caller* still exists is because the guy running it is one of the very rare conservative intellectuals who understands business," Carlson told *The Wall Street Journal* in 2020. "There's no magic secret, as far as I know, other than [Patel] keeps costs in line with revenue."

That same year, Carlson stepped down from the *Daily Caller* to focus on his Fox News show; with its own website attracting some 117 million visitors a month, Fox News saw Carlson's involvement with the *Daily Caller* as a conflict of interest. Patel bought out Carlson's one-third interest in the company, which left the *Daily Caller* the largest digital media company wholly owned by a racial minority.

CHAPTER THIRTEEN

Tucker Carlson Tonight is to go on live in eight minutes and, civilian that I am, I'm nervous he won't make it.

Carlson's executive producer, Justin Wells, isn't bothered in the least; he assures me this is perfectly normal. It's now 7:53 p.m. and, sure enough, Carlson bounds out of the pool house, still buttoning his shirt, fresh out of the shower, having filed his monologue just before that. The dogs leap off the bed and follow him through the sliding glass door.

"Oops, better take a leak first," Carlson says. Unzipping trow, he relieves himself on a bed of red anthurium next to the pool.

"He has to do this every night," Wells says drily.

Carlson looks over his shoulder mid-stream. "Want to hear my favorite joke? When God was almost done creating Adam and Eve, he said to them: 'Alright I am almost done with you. I have two more gifts I can give you.' Adam and Eve ask, 'What are they?' God says, 'The first one is the gift of peeing while standing up.' Adam shoves Eve out of the way, 'Me! Me! Me! I want to pee standing up!' he shouts. So, God grants him the gift of peeing upright and Adam starts wizzing all over the Garden of Eden. Then he pauses and turns to God and asks, 'Wait, what was the other gift?' And God turns to Eve and says, 'You get multiple orgasms,'" Carlson laughs. "I love that joke, I tell it to my wife all the time — I say, I have to use what I got!"

Tucker leans on Wells, whom he calls "an amazing journalist, old school," and someone with whom "I am completely in sync on everything."

But the executive producer confides that at first, Carlson "didn't quite know what to make of me. He was like, '*Is the gay guy really conservative? Is he going to undermine me? All my producers always have.*' I'd say it was about six months before he learned to trust me, and after we launched the show together it's been a partnership ever since."

In addition to drawing them closer, their time side by side in the bunker taking enemy fire has left them with a treasure trove of shared anecdotes, including a few of the post-frat-boy variety. At one point, Carlson shows me a framed photograph of himself and Wells seated at a sunny table, smiling at the camera through the glare of the window behind them. A plated dessert sits between them and both clutch forks.

"I love that picture," Carlson says, "I love that day. We were in Finland, in the presidential palace in Helsinki, where Trump was having a summit with Putin."

"And they were preparing the dinner for them," picks up Wells, "and we broke into the kitchen."

"They were putting their desserts on a tray," says Tucker, "and we said we were with President Putin and we'd like the desserts, and we went to this side room and ate their desserts."

Sean Hannity was also in the room, adds the producer, so when they went to get a second helping, "we brought some back to Sean, and said, 'Here you go, here's Putin's dessert.'" He laughs.

"He wouldn't eat it," Carlson says. "He was afraid because it was Putin's. But we did. And we were so happy. Look at the happiness in that photo. We're in the middle of eating Vladimir Putin's dessert."

Of course, to be part of Carlson's inner circle by definition makes Wells a target in his own right. Behind-the-scenes staff rarely are the subject of public scrutiny unless they seek the spotlight or have been convicted of a crime. Though Wells has never done either, the normal rules were suspended because of his association with Tucker. Last year his husband, Ryan, suffered a seizure that resulted in aphasia, leaving him unable to verbalize beyond one-word responses. As Ryan lay in intensive care, a veteran gay-rights activist named Michelangelo Signorile stumbled upon the bombshell that Tucker Carlson's executive producer was an openly gay man and released an all-points bulletin to the community. Wells, he wrote, has "helped promulgate the kind of hate that leads to violence," and "aided the extremists who deny that sense of safety and liberation to every future generation of queer people." Signorile's post, titled "The powerful gay man behind Tucker Carlson's bloodcurdling hate," was dutifully picked up by left-wing groups. "Wells runs the entire Tucker Carlson operation," it continued, "and is responsible for imprinting the Tucker Carlson brand, which is all about emboldening white heterosexual male grievance, furthering the racist conspiracy theory of 'replacement theory' and pushing an increasingly virulent anti-LGBTQ agenda."

Though it obviously came at a bad time, Wells, like Tucker, has developed an impressively thick skin. "He still tweets about me every week," notes Wells, with a chuckle.

While in Florida, Wells and Ryan are staying in Tucker's home — the same room where Mike Tyson and his wife recently stayed when the boxer came down to do *Tucker Carlson Today* — "The room Mike Tyson had sex in," jokes Tucker. Justin and Ryan have been married for over a decade and are beloved members of the Carlson family. Ryan and Susie seem particularly close. Since the seizure, Susie helps complete his sentences. She asks what he wants to say and he's able to respond "yes," or "no."

Now Tucker, Wells and I pile into a pink golf cart parked in the gravel driveway heading for the studio. Carlson is driving, I'm in the passenger seat, and Wells is perched on the back gripping the handrails. This is Carlson's personal, modified golf cart — he removed the roof.

"It's the one requirement for my commute," he tells me, "that I can see the sky."

For the six months he's in Maine, he commutes every night, even if it's raining, by boat. "That's something that always makes me laugh about global warming," he says, and does laugh, this idea that: *I am in charge of the weather*. What I love about the weather is I'm *not* in charge of it."

Carlson floors it, the gravel crunches, and we swerve onto a golf-cart path parallel to the main road. "Isn't this great?" Carlson shouts above the whirl and rushing air. "I have my entire script in my head and my best lines come to me on this drive."

It's a slightly chilly, late-February evening. This part of Florida — colonial, muted, understated with WASPy sensibility, working-class locals, and an appreciation for eccentrics — is more Cape Cod in the tropics than the opulence and stuffiness of Palm Beach, 170 miles due east on the Atlantic coast, where Rush Limbaugh made his home and former president Donald Trump currently resides. Commercial and sport fishing, mainly tarpon, along with phosphate mining, which ended in the 1970s, formerly sustained the local economy. Today, second-, third-, and fourth-generation fishermen hobnob with the winter residents, and, for all its wealth, the place feels like it values community over venture capital.

We dart past the Gasparilla Inn, a towering, sandy-yellow hotel built in 1911 in what's known as the Frame Vernacular style. Before the 1930s, fresh water had to be brought into the hotel by railcar. Early guests of the Gasparilla included tycoons J.P. Morgan, Henry du Pont, Henry Ford, and Harvey Firestone. In the year before Carlson found a space to use as a full-time local studio, he broadcast his show from room 308 at the Gasparilla. The ten-foot-by-twelve-foot hotel room was so cramped, Wells informs me, that "you couldn't breathe or fart without it being heard on camera." Still, Carlson welcomed local people to watch the show, as he still does, and in the tight quarters they would plaster themselves against a wall trying not to move or make a sound.

We pull into the parking lot, where an ununiformed security guard greets us, and step into the permanent studio. It isn't all that much bigger than its predecessor, roughly the size of a Manhattan studio apartment, but it does the trick. The set is a near-perfect reproduction of the one in Maine, only the decorative knickknacks on the wall differing slightly. The pinewood veneer and curved acrylic desk will also be familiar to viewers of *Tucker Carlson Today*, the long-form interview show he hosted on Fox Nation; while with the network, for half the year, from Florida, Tucker recorded three episodes back-to-back every Tuesday afternoon. Although he did both shows from the same seat, TV magic in the guise of a monitor behind him gave the impression of two different venues, the illusion shattered only on the rare occasions he had an in-studio guest seated to his right on the nightly show.

Between the three Tucker Carlson shows, the staff was about twenty-five people. "We built an amazing team," says Wells, "and a big reason it works is this close-knit group of people he trusts. And it's mutual — all the crew people and staff love Tucker. He's not a screamer, it's just not who he is, and no one is trying to undermine anyone else, everyone knows what they're doing. I've seen every kind of TV anchor — local news, network news, and I can't tell you how unusual that is."

Wells saw his job as executive producer as "driving what Tucker's skilled at and what he believes. If he's not passionate about something, it doesn't work. But we'll cover some niche topic that wouldn't work for anyone else — like the importance of great architecture — that wouldn't work for a typical cable host and does for him because he's so passionate about it. Of course, he's good at funny, too, which a lot of cable-news hosts aren't. If we didn't live in such a divisive world, he could be a game-show host on the side. Actually, during the *Crossfire* years he did do some pilots for game shows; one was a *Jeopardy!*-type show. Sure, he's a journalist, but he knows how to perform for the camera. Even at dinner parties." He laughs. "He's compelling in any environment when the lights are on," Wells says.

The "audience" for tonight's taping — three women in their eighties, two American snowbirds along with a visiting friend from Australia — are already seated in folding chairs along the wall opposite Carlson's news desk. The two locals are dressed in shades of pink and pastel. They have refined Southern drawls and tall, yellow hair. Carlson greets them with familiarity and a beaming smile; they embrace. Carlson says he's looking forward to fishing with one of their sons next weekend.

However, there's a tinge of awkwardness; Carlson's monologue that night explores the failings of advanced age, specifically pertaining to President Joe Biden. As a producer wrangles a tie around his neck — there's a rack near the bathroom with about two hundred slightly varied, diagonal-striped neckties in navies, greens, yellows, and reds — Carlson prepares the ladies, with a hint of apology, for what he's about to say on air about old people. The ladies couldn't be less bothered; they're simply delighted to be here and they, too, think Joe Biden is too old to be president.

The first order of business is tonight's music. Carlson curates a playlist each night that's heard internally during commercial breaks. Guests waiting to go live also hear the music from whatever studio across the country, or world, where they happen to be. "I'd like to start the evening with Miko Marks, 'Feel Like Going Home,'" Carlson tells New York. "Then let's play 'Hard Working Man' by Marcus King, which is another great fucking song, then let's do Sharon Jones's cover of 'Midnight Rider.' It's a fifty-year-old song and she adds horns and a blues inflection to it. It's just amazing. And I'm on a Sturgill Simpson kick lately. How about 'Paradise' by Sturgill Simpson? Another great song."

As this is happening, Carlson is simultaneously fielding input from Alex McCaskill, a producer in New York speaking into his earpiece, as well as making eye contact with the octogenarians against the wall, when abruptly he booms: "Good evening and welcome to *Tucker Carlson Tonight!*" and it takes a jarring moment to realize he's just gone live and millions of eyes are suddenly upon him.

And he is off into his monologue.

"Here is the main thing you need to know about Joe Biden. He is eighty years old. He was born in 1942 in the first half of the last century. The year Biden was born, only 36 percent of American households had a telephone. Nearly half of them did not have indoor plumbing. Joe Biden turned eighty last November. This fall, he will be eighty-one. If Biden were to serve a second full term as president, he would be eighty-six years old. In other words, four years from ninety.

"These are not trivial facts about Joe Biden. These are the central facts of Joe Biden's life. Joe Biden's age defines him and all of us. That's true for every person. 'Age is just a number,' you will hear people say. But they are lying to themselves. Age is more than a number. Age is an expression of the core biological reality of human existence . . ."

Carlson's monologues read so well that Fox News used to publish nearly each one word-for-word as a column the following day on its website, where they usually rank at the top of the site's traffic. "So much goes into those A-block scripts," Wells tells me, "people don't realize how creative the process is, how much he's drawing from when he writes them — and while the sound bites and stuff are put together for him, he truly writes that A-block.

"At his core, I think he always just wanted to be a writer. He can tell good writing from bad writing in two seconds, and he's very specific in his word choices, which is a big part of what makes the monologues great."

Tucker Carlson Tonight premiered on November 14, 2016. At the time, Carlson was still living in Washington, D.C., and the show's original home was at D.C.'s Fox News bureau, with production support coming from Fox HQ in New York. The show was created to replace *On the Record*, which had been taken over by Brit Hume after Greta Van Susteren's abrupt departure from Fox.

Tucker Carlson Tonight premiered with 3.7 million viewers, making it the network's most watched telecast for the year in the 7:00 p.m. timeslot. Even at that early stage, Carlson drew 750,000 viewers in the coveted twenty-five to fifty-four age demographic, more than CNN and MSNBC combined.

The ratings were such that on January 9, 2017, the show was moved into the more desirable 9:00 p.m. timeslot, recently vacated by *The Kelly File* when Megyn Kelly left Fox for NBC News.

"In less than two months, Tucker has taken cable news by storm with his spirited interviews and consistently strong perfor-mance," crowed Rupert Murdoch, owner of News Corp, Fox's parent company, in a statement at the time. "Viewers have overwhelmingly responded to the show and we look forward to him being a part of Fox News' powerful primetime line-up."

Fox's primetime shuffle continued with the departure of Bill O'Reilly just a few months later, in April 2017.

The O'Reilly Factor had of course been a resounding success. Fox's flagship show, it was the top cable-news show for 106 consecutive weeks, peaking at 3.1 million viewers. Still, although O'Reilly maintained his top position in ratings, he'd been slipping, his nightly viewership having dropped to an average 2.1 million, with a median age of seventy-two years old. When *The New York Times* reported in 2017 that O'Reilly had paid a $13 million settlement to five women who had accused him of sexual harassment, in short order, nearly sixty companies dropped ads from *The O'Reilly Factor*.

Amid the scandal, O'Reilly announced he'd be taking a long-planned two-week vacation, and five days before his scheduled April 24 return to the air, Fox News issued a statement. "After a thorough and careful review of the allegations, the Company and Bill O'Reilly have agreed that Bill O'Reilly will not be returning to the Fox News Channel." It added that Tucker Carlson would move into the 8:00 p.m. timeslot the following Monday, April 24, with Dana Perino and Greg Gutfeld guest hosting the remaining three episodes of the *Factor*.

During O'Reilly's "vacation," with guest host Perino filling in, the ratings in the timeslot had fallen 26 percent. They picked up the first night Carlson took the slot, and rose steadily over the following six years.

"Nicotine break!" exclaims Carlson, the moment he goes into his first commercial break, popping a packet of Zyn (six milligram, spearmint) into his mouth. "Anyone else like some nicotine?"

A producer comes over to fix his hair, and he says "Let me do it — nicotine spit, gives it a nice sheen." Spitting in his hand, he flattens the unruly fluffy bit.

Taking the seat to Carlson's right, in the chair where an in-studio guest would be, Wells tells me about the time a third-party contractor recorded the chit-chat between commercial breaks. Carlson had recently undergone emergency back surgery and was on a course of powerful opioids for the pain, and he was telling the crew about the experience of taking the drugs.

"That was one of the most intense experiences of my life," Carlson said on the full audio. "They hit me up with such a huge dose of Dilaudid, which is more powerful than morphine, that I had trouble breathing. Scared the shit out of me. Didn't have any effect at all. And then all night, I lay there. The nurse finally upped my dosage of dilaudid to the point where every eight minutes I hit it and it was like getting shot. Just like bam, feel it hit me, and it didn't touch the pain. They gave me fentanyl this morning, that did not cure it — they gave me intravenous fentanyl," he said. "And they gave me all kinds of other shit. I was like, 'Fine, go for it.' And then it only ended when they gave me propofol, and I went out. Then I woke up and I was like, I felt totally fine. I haven't taken a single Advil.

"It was super deep. And I just haven't had those feelings since I was in a plane crash twenty years ago this month. I've never had those feelings. I'm always like 'Yeah I'm gonna die, I don't care.' And I mean it. But last night I was like, 'Oh shit.' Fear — just like anxiety. People who have anxiety, that's what I felt. And it was from those drugs. And they extinguish the spirit within you. And they make you feel like you're running away. You're hiding. It's so fucking deep. I'm lying in bed with filthy dog toys on my pillow, and it doesn't bother me. And I'm not that way. Like I am a fucking — in real life, I wash the sheets every day. I'm that guy. I shower every day."

In short, it was a discussion about the horrors of opioids. But it was edited to make Carlson sound like a drug addict, and leaked to the press.

"We know who it was," Wells says now, of the technician who stole the audio. "We're thinking of suing him."

In the next block of tonight's show, Florida Governor Ron DeSantis is teed up on the remote feed. While he's appearing to promote his new book, it's no secret that it's also a quasi-campaign appearance, as Republicans are abuzz about the likelihood of a presidential run. It is apparent that Team DeSantis watches Carlson's show closely and that the governor sometimes takes cues from the most influential talk-show host on the air. This past fall, DeSantis further endeared himself to the Republican base by airlifting migrants to toney Martha's Vineyard. It was a vastly entertaining political stunt that, more to the point, highlighted the progressives' appalling hypocrisy on the border issue — and he got the idea from *Tucker Carlson Tonight*.

Texas Governor Greg Abbott had been first out of the gate, in the summer initiating a bussing program that sent thousands of illegal migrants from the Texas border to Democrat-controlled, self-described sanctuary cities like Chicago, New York, and Washington, D.C. But Carlson observed that the bussing program wasn't going far enough.

"The bigger problem is a lack of diversity," he said on his July 26 broadcast. "Immigrants are supposed to make America more diverse. In practice, they initially head to places that are already pretty diverse. The party of diversity is strongly, overwhelmingly, led by people who prefer all-white neighborhoods for themselves and their families."

"There are an awful lot of Democratic donors in Aspen, Colorado. What do we do about this? Imagine an Aspen airlift, a national effort to rescue the people of Aspen from the suffocating prison of their own whiteness. Instead of food and coal and medicine, the Biden administration could deliver an even more essential life-saving commodity, and that's diversity into the cultural wasteland of Pitkin County, Colorado, which if you can believe it, as of tonight, is only one half of one percent black. Into that, Joe Biden could deposit Haitians and Somalis and Congolese — hundreds and hundreds of thousands of them — Guatemalans, Guineans, Algerians, the entire population of the Cape Verde Islands. We can do that. We're America. And why stop with those countries? As of tonight, there are still four million people living in the impoverished state of Oaxaca, Mexico. Do you care about them? We do, because we're good people. So why shouldn't a quarter of all Oaxacans move to Aspen by next ski season. And to be clear, not move there to run the chairlifts at Snowmass, move there to ride the chairlifts at Snowmass to benefit fully from the economic bounty of that isolated blindingly white mountain community we call Aspen. Is there anything more American than that? Next stop on the equity train has got to be Martha's Vineyard. It's a natural."

Carlson went on that the Vineyard, where former president Barack Obama recently purchased a $12 million waterfront compound, has "effectively zero diversity, which means zero strength. They are begging for more diversity. Why not send migrants there in huge numbers? Let's start with 300,000 and move up from there."

Over the following weeks, Carlson repeated his call to send migrants to Martha's Vineyard — until, in September, two planes carrying forty-eight illegal migrants from Venezuela stealthily flew from Ron DeSantis's Florida to the Vineyard, where posters distributed by Martha's Vineyard's Main Street Alliance proclaimed "All Are Welcome Here"; and "We stand with IMMIGRANTS, with REFUGEES, with INDIGENOUS PEOPLES, and with PEOPLE OF ALL FAITHS."

Sure enough, within forty-eight hours, the Massachusetts National Guard had been deployed to escort the migrants off the island, and send them to the less hospitable environs of Joint Base Cape Cod.

"They enriched us," one unembarrassed resident had the nerve to tell reporters after gratefully waving the unwelcome Venezuelans goodbye. "We're happy to help them on their journey."

Though the mainstream press labored to make the best of a humiliating and all-too-revealing situation — CNN fawned that the migrants "left an indelible mark on their accidental hosts in this isolated enclave known as a summer playground for former U.S. presidents, celebrities and billionaires" — these were the exactly sort of entitled and hypocritical white liberals decent people loathe, and the nation was laughing at them. To dispel criticism of the island's demographics, *The Boston Globe* ran the headline, "Martha's Vineyard was portrayed as rich, white, and elite, but there's another side to the island." The only example the paper found of the island's diversity, however, was a thirty-six-year-old black immigrant from Jamaica who lived in Falmouth, on the mainland, and commuted to the island to work as a bank teller.

Indeed, the stunt provided irrefutable evidence of the smugness that defines America's ruling class, perfectly validating the things Carlson had been preaching about for years.

Of course, such *lèse majesté* couldn't go unpunished; Democrat leaders wanted a scalp, and *The New York Times* was on the case. The migrants had been tricked, declared the paper of record. The flights were a "clandestine mission," and possibly criminal. Documentary filmmaker Ken Burns appeared on CNN in his bad toupee, comparing the Martha's Vineyard airlift to the actions of Hitler in Nazi Germany. "This is coming straight out of the authoritarian playbook," he said. "What we find in all our films is that the themes that we engage in the past are present today . . . And so when you look at the story that we're telling of the U.S. and the Holocaust, you understand that the time to save a democracy is before it's lost."

In a letter to Biden's Attorney General, Merrick Garland, Democratic California Governor Gavin Newsom urged the Justice Department to investigate Ron DeSantis on kidnapping charges. A Democratic state lawmaker representing Miami-Dade County filed a lawsuit against DeSantis, alleging the stunt was an illegitimate use of funds that violated Florida law.

But the damage had been done — which is to say, the entire affair was a huge win for DeSantis, governor of the state where, in his catchphrase, "woke goes to die."

At the time, probably because the journalists involved watch MSNBC, it was little understood that the whole thing was Carlson's idea. Had it been, there might well have been another call for advertiser boycotts of his show, and possibly even a criminal investigation. For immigration is the topic that seems to get Carlson in trouble the most. As Wells tells it, there were a couple of times when it was feared the show might actually get pulled off the air for its content.

The most dangerous of these controversies followed Carlson's December 13, 2018 broadcast, in which he'd used the word "dirtier" in discussing the invasion of migrants at the Southern border.

"We've got a moral obligation to admit the world's poor, they tell us, even if it makes our own country poorer, dirtier, and more divided," Carlson declared, accompanied by images of migrants in garbage-strewn Tijuana encampments as they awaited entry to the U.S.

In the maelstrom of negative press that ensued, Tucker was roundly accused of racism, and advertisers reacted to the coordinated hit with panic. A number departed from the show, including Bowflex, the insurance company Pacific Life, SmileDirectClub, the jobs website Indeed, the finance website NerdWallet, and the design marketplace Minted.

The Monday following the controversy, Carlson doubled down, likening the criticism and loss of ad revenue to an attack on freedom of speech. He then dug deeper into the issue of litter and illegal immigration. "Take a trip to our southwestern deserts if you don't believe it. Thanks to illegal immigration, huge swaths of the region are covered with garbage and waste that degrade the soil and kill wildlife."

"The Arizona Department of Environment Quality estimates that each illegal border crosser leaves six to eight pounds of trash during the journey into our country. If you're interested in more detail, look at the website they've created, it's called Arizona Border Trash. It's dedicated to highlighting and cleaning up the thousands of tons of garbage strewn across Arizona by immigrants every year," he went on. "Illegal immigration comes at a huge cost to our environment. The Government Accountability Office put it this way: 'Illegal border activity on federal lands not only threatens people, but endangered species and the land itself. Illegal aliens and smugglers have destroyed cactus and other sensitive vegetation that can take decades to recover, including habitat for endangered species. One land management official described another federal property on Arizona's border as so unsafe and with resources so destroyed that it is now primarily used for illegal activities and no longer visited by the general public."

Despite murmurs from unidentified sources within Fox telling liberal media that he had "finally crossed some kind of line," and *The New York Times* wondering "what price he might pay," Carlson's refusal to bend a knee stood him in good stead. After a week or so the story melted away.

Three years later, the usual actors once more launched an advertiser boycott of the show based on Carlson's comments on immigration. On September 22, 2021, he played an old clip of Joe Biden, as vice president, praising the impending loss of a white majority in the U.S. "An unrelenting stream of immigration," said Biden. "Nonstop, nonstop. Folks like me who are Caucasian, of European descent, for the first time in 2017 we'll be an absolute minority in the United States of America. Absolute minority. Fewer than 50 percent of the people in America from then and on will be white European stock. That's not a bad thing. That's a source of our strength."

"Why?" responded Carlson on air. "To change the racial mix of the country. That's the reason. To reduce the political power of people whose ancestors lived here, and dramatically increase the proportion of Americans newly arrived from the Third World. And then Biden went further and said that non-white DNA is the source of our strength. Imagine saying that. This is the language of eugenics. It's horrifying. But there's a reason Biden said it. In political terms, this policy is sometimes called the Great Replacement — the replacement of legacy Americans, with more obedient people from faraway countries."

The Great Replacement theory is thought to have been inspired by a French dystopian novel called *The Camp of Saints*, which depicts the mass immigration of people from the Third World, supported by journalists and politicians, leading to the destruction of France. Since its publication in the seventies, many have come to see the novel as prophetic. The book was said to be a favorite of Trump advisors Steve Bannon and Stephen Miller.

But the subject was all but untouchable, and after Carlson cited the Great Replacement as the means by which progressives intended to overwhelm traditional Republican-leaning white voters, the Anti-Defamation League spearheaded an effort to get him fired. Ignoring Carlson's point about the threat of unchecked immigration to democratic norms, the ADL asserted it was such thinking that had been responsible for the mass killing three years earlier of Jewish congregants at a synagogue in Pittsburgh that left eleven dead, as well as other such attacks worldwide, including the consecutive terrorist attacks on two mosques in Christchurch, New Zealand, where the shooter's manifesto was entitled, "The Great Replacement". A subsequent shooting at a Walmart in El Paso, Texas, that killed twenty-three Latino shoppers was also said to be inspired by the theory.In response to the calls for his firing, Lachlan Murdoch, chief executive of the Fox Corporation, wrote: "Mr. Carlson decried and rejected replacement theory. As Mr. Carlson himself stated, 'White replacement theory? No, no, this is a voting rights question.'"

Conservative politicians and activists followed suit. On September 23, Turning Point USA founder Charlie Kirk declared on his show that the Biden administration's immigration policy "is about bringing in voters that they like and, honestly, diminishing and decreasing white demographics in America." The next day, Republican Congressman Brian Babin of Texas said on Fox News, "They want to change America, they want to replace the American electorate with third-world immigrants that are coming in illegally." Florida Congressman Matt Gaetz tweeted, "@TuckerCarlson is CORRECT about Replacement Theory as he explains what is happening to America. The ADL is a racist organization."

After the uproar died down, Megyn Kelly asked Carlson on her podcast how he felt when "sure enough the ADL comes after you."

"The ADL?" Carlson said, laughing. "Fuck them." The ADL, "was a noble organization that had a very specific goal, which was to fight anti-Semitism, and that's a virtuous goal. They were pretty successful over the years. Now it's operated by a guy who's just an apparatchik of the Democratic party."

"It's very corrosive for someone to take the residual moral weight of an organization that he inherited and use it for a party," he continued. "So, the Great Replacement theory is, in fact, not a theory. It's something that the Democrats brag about constantly, up to and including the president. And in one sentence, it's this: 'Rather than convince the current population that our policies are working, and they should vote for us as a result, we can't be bothered to do that. We're instead going to change the composition of the population and bring in people who will vote for us.' So, there isn't actually inherently a racial component to it, and it's nothing to do with anti-Semitism."

"They target us because we, by far, across all platforms, have the most eyeballs," asserts Wells, noting that the show reached a far broader demographic than most shows on Fox, which generally draws those Rush Limbaugh used to refer to as "seasoned citizens." "Tucker is not like your grandparents' Fox News, and I think that threatens people a lot. That he can relate to young men, women. We have a lot of fun, too, along with the substance, makes us an even bigger threat. The left thinks we're grooming younger people, not all of them conservatives, to think differently, and that scares the shit out of them. It's scary because he's making a case based on facts and offers intellectual value. Trump had a lot of great ideas, but in that sense, Tucker offers something Trump doesn't have."

He adds that this is why so many wonder if Tucker plans to run for president, something he says he has no interest in. Still, "I think that's why they go after Tucker; they want to take him out before he gains even more traction. So they'll take twenty seconds out of a carefully crafted twenty-minute piece to make him look bad. But it hasn't worked, because even if people disagree with the premise, when you watch the totality of it, the arguments he makes are pretty indisputable. So, they take one little thing, like 'immigrants are dirty,' and turn that into a boycott."

Of course, the hit jobs kept coming. Among the most ambitious of recent vintage was a sprawling, nine-thousand-word May 4, 2022 piece in *The New York Times*. Beginning on page one and going on forever inside, among other things it took the curious tack of trying to portray Carlson — many of whose harshest critics will at least agree has been remarkably steady in his views over the decades — as shifting with the political winds for career advantage. For one thing, the paper claimed he'd once been an immigration proponent, but had switched to mine the "racist," nativist sentiment in the Republican Party. For another, it asserted that "Like many up-and-coming conservative writers in the 1990s, Mr. Carlson had vaguely libertarian politics — or, at least, a vaguely libertarian sensibility."

In fact, typically, it was the *Times* that was being disingenuous. There is no evidence that Carlson was ever sympathetic to open borders. Colleagues at the *Daily Caller* told the *Times* Carlson was "known to his staff as an immigration hawk; in office debates he would sometimes invoke Lewiston as a kind of personal turning point." Lewiston, Maine, population 37,000, is less than an hour down the road from his childhood summer home. In 2000, refugees from West Africa began settling there and today number nearly 10 percent of the population, making it home to one of the largest Somali communities in the U.S. This has led to dramatic spikes in crime, civil discordance, and striking shifts in political power.

As for his alleged former sympathetic view of libertarianism, twenty years ago Carlson wrote in *New York* magazine that "The average Republican views the average libertarian as a crackpot with a weird personal life. The average Republican is onto something. Libertarians tend to be odd. By definition, they're cranky and non-conformist. They like theories. They dress poorly. They don't follow instructions well," he wrote. "On the other hand, politics informed by libertarian instincts — the libertarian spirit rather than actual libertarianism — is a good thing. It has been a winner for Republicans."

He continued: "At the heart of almost every GOP campaign is a libertarian theme, usually expressed in anti-Washington terms: 'The professional politicians back in Washington want to tell you how to live your life. Elect me to stop them.' It's a message that people who wouldn't consider supporting a bona fide pro-heroin, pro-prostitution libertarian can embrace. It works."

"Tucker is very resilient. Every time he's gotten the hit, I think he's stronger for it," Wells tells me when the evening's show is over.

"I don't think you can cancel Tucker, it's impossible, whether he's at Fox or elsewhere."

He pauses, then adds wryly, with what would turn out to be impressive clairvoyance, "I say that now, but maybe I'll regret it."

On the ride back home in the golf cart, Carlson is thinking about something else that with coming events will prove invaluable: perspective.

"The stars are such a persistent reminder we're not in charge," he offers offhandedly, indicating the night sky through the open roof. "I mean, the underlying message of the TV show, the message of *every* TV show, is I'm omnipotent. That I'm a God. Take one hour out of your day and listen to my stupid opinions on whatever is happening because I'm right and you're wrong. It has to be the message or else no one watches." He pauses. "The problem is, if you start to believe that after a while you become a miserable, horrible, human being. So I make sure I see this on my way home, three hundred sixty-five days a year. Because when you look up and there are all these lights . . . wow. I'm totally insignificant. What I do won't change the position of a single light in the sky. All my dramas mean nothing. I share those dramas with a million years of ancestors who shared the same dramas. They weren't on television, but they're the same dramas: Power, love, nature, sex. And they'll all be there when I'm gone."

CHAPTER
FOURTEEN

T hat's one of my favorite words," Carlson is saying. "It's super naughty, but it's to the point. It's 'Break glass in case of emergency!'"

The word in question is "cunt."

We're having this conversation because Carlson's use of the forbidden syllable is at this moment making screaming headlines. Hours ago, his private text messages were made public as part of discovery in Dominion Voting Systems' $1.6 billion defamation lawsuit against Fox News, the company alleging Fox falsely claimed their voting machines were insecure during the 2020 presidential election. In one text, Carlson called Trump lawyer Sidney Powell, who pushed the claims against Dominion at the time, a liar and a "cunt."

"'Fuck' is so overused it's lost all its power and meaning," adds Tucker now. "It doesn't have the same impact anymore."

As we talk it over in his Florida pool house, he shows little sense of concern. His four spaniels are with us. Dave, the black one, sits on his lap. Meg, Alice, and Brookie rest at his feet. Brookie is geriatric, confused, possibly blind, and for that reason seems to be the favorite. Dave (also female) is ornerier.

The pool house, encompassing just a bed, closet, and bathroom, indeed feels like a refuge from the chaotic world beyond. Tucker and Susie, live here, leaving the main house for visiting children and guests, and the dogs sleep with them. Outside there's what Carlson calls the writing garden — a sliver of a backyard lined with banana trees, palms, Norfolk Island pine, bougainvillea, and varieties of begonia, as well as a freestanding sauna and an outdoor shower.

"Maine is great because he has lots of space," Susie has told me. "The whole state is unpopulated, he can get in his truck and go anywhere. But I need some social life, friends to go to dinner with, so he does this for me.

That's why I've tried to create a space that's as peaceful as possible, with lots of greenery, because down here it is really the only private space he has."

Needless to say, what Tucker's said about Powell is being much discussed elsewhere. The media is of course taking it as evidence of a toxic work environment at Fox and proof of Carlson's own inherent misogyny.

Potentially even more damaging are Carlson's comments in the texts about President Trump. As votes were being counted after Election Day 2020, Carlson, concerned viewers were turning away from Fox after the network called Arizona early for Joe Biden, exchanged texts with Fox producer Alex Pfeiffer. "Trump has a pretty low rate at success in his business ventures," Pfeiffer wrote.

"That's for sure," replied Carlson. "All of them fail. What he's good at is destroying things. He's the undisputed world champion of that."

In a later exchange with another staff member, Carlson called Trump's decision to not attend Joe Biden's inauguration, "Hard to believe. So destructive. It's disgusting."

In text messages dated January 7, 2021, one day after election-integrity protestors entered the U.S. Capitol building — the infamous "Insurrection," as Democrats branded it — Carlson wrote to Pfeiffer, "Trump has two weeks left. Once he's out, he becomes incalculably less powerful, even in the minds of his supporters," and, "He's a demonic force, a destroyer. But he's not going to destroy us. I've been thinking about this every day for four years."

"You're right. I don't want to let him destroy me either. [REDACTED]. The Trump anger spiral is vicious," Pfeiffer responded.

"That's for sure. Deadly. It almost consumed me in November when Sidney Powell attacked us. It was very difficult to regain emotional control, but I knew I had to. We've got two weeks left. We can do this," Carlson wrote back.

Carlson's enemies spent the ensuing hours painting Carlson as a TrumpWorld fraud, talking from both sides of his mouth. They were positively giddy at the prospect this might sever Carlson from his audience.

Astute Tucker-watchers, however, knew that even during Trump's presidency, and in stark contrast to almost everyone else in the media, berserk haters and cheerleaders alike, Carlson rarely talked on his show about the man himself. He was among the many who seemed to like Trumpism while studiously keeping Trump at arm's length.

"Do I like Trump? I love Trump," Carlson tells me now. "But there are many levels to Trump. He was a completely ineffectual president. He couldn't manage my household. He's not a manager, and that's very frustrating to watch. The federal government is the largest organization in history, there's never been a larger organization — millions of people, the largest budget, largest workforce, incredibly complex — I don't know how any person can control it. So that was very frustrating to watch, extremely frustrating, infuriating to watch his stated agenda get subverted by people who work for him. It was crazy. Like watching someone's kids burn his own house down and he can't do anything about it. I really hated watching that and I was mad about it.

"So, there's that; there's Trump on the level of manager. But Trump on the level of guy? To have dinner with Trump is one of the great joys in the world. If you were to assemble a list of people to have dinner with, Trump would be in the top spot. He's beyond belief. He's a television figure. He was the number-one star at NBC. So how do you get to that? By being an incredibly amusing, charming, dynamic person. Trump at that level is just absolutely the best. So funny, so unbelievably eccentric and monomaniacal in a hilarious way. So nice, too. I always think of Trump as like an innkeeper. You go to any property that Trump owns and he immediately assumes the role of the Greek innkeeper at the bed and breakfast in Mykonos, showing you around. *And over here we have the best swimming pool in Mykonos!* He's standing in the doorway when you walk in, he leads you around. He's unbelievable. That's just in his blood. It's who he is. In the end, Trump is just the maître d', a wonderful host. Funny, outrageous, absolutely on his own planet. And I have a love for people like that. I grew up around people like that.

"I don't think Trump is a political person at all. I don't think he understands politics that well. I think he thinks he does; I don't think he does. I'm saying that as someone who doesn't understand politics at all, but I know that I don't. I don't have a tactile sense of that. What does it take to assemble a presidential campaign? How would you do that? I just don't know, and I don't want to know. I don't find it appealing. That's so far out of my love that I don't want anything to do with it. I think Trump is very much the same. He's just a guy who wanted the prestige of being president, was frustrated with how things were going, and just decided he was going to wing it and see what happens. But I think Trump's execution mistake was imagining he's a political tactician, which he's certainly not, at all. He's way out of his depth in that.

"I'm a huge believer in people staying in their lane. Identify our strengths, orient your life around maximizing those and minimizing your weaknesses. I tell my children all the time: You're good at some things and you're not good at others. Don't lie to yourself. Figure out what you're good at, emphasize that, build your life around that. You cannot be whatever you want to be. You were given a bundle of strengths and weaknesses at birth and roll with those. A stonecutter goes along the preexisting form. You see a crack in the stone, that's what you're cutting. You didn't make the crack; you find it and you go with it. And I think all people are like that.

"It's frustrating to see Trump do things he's not good at, when he's good at so much. And one of the things he's so good at is having dinner. I don't think your behavior at dinner is a small thing. It's a huge thing. Meals are really important, among the more important things that we do, eating with other people. What did Jesus do the night before he died? Being entertaining, connecting people, learning something, talking, listening, enjoying. Those are not just things you do when you have nothing else to do. That's a focus of your day. We're super serious about dinner in our family."

There is also a personal element to Carlson's feelings about Donald Trump. Back in 2018, three days after the attack by Antifa radicals on the Carlsons' Washington home, Susie got a call from President Trump on her cell phone. "He said, 'I'm thinking about you,'" Susie tells me, "'I'm so sorry that this happened, and do you want me to come stand at your front door?' And I was like, *No! No!*," Susie laughs. "*Not a good plan! But thank you.* And he said, 'I just want you to know, Susie, there's a lot of love in this world.' And I have thought about that sentence so many times. It's become kind of a mantra to me. If I get down, or if I feel that Tucker's under attack, or there's negativity, not just about him but anywhere in the world, I remind myself what he said, which is there's a lot of love in the world. And there is. And that's what you have to focus on. You know, that's what I try to do."

In July 2022 a photo of Tucker with Trump at Trump's golf club in Bedminster, New Jersey, went viral. In the photo the two are on a balcony watching a golf tournament. Carlson is laughing as Trump leans into him, whispering something. I ask Carlson if he remembers what was so funny. "I do. He was talking about the beer girls. 'Look at those beer girls? Can you believe they have legs like that? You can't make legs like that, that's genetics! The human genome explains that!'" Carlson laughs. "That's what he was saying, and I love that. You're telling me something that amuses the hell out of me. Because it's rooted in truth and it's unexpected. I'm the perfect audience for that." He pauses. "I'd actually never been to a golf tournament before; I'm not a golfer. I'm left-handed and have no coordination. I grew up hunting and fishing. But, like I say, Trump feels a moral obligation to entertain the people in his world. He's the patriarch and everyone in his orbit needs to be entertained by him. And I agree that's absolutely an obligation the head man has, and people who don't live up to it are falling down on the job.

"I remember very vividly every meal I've had with Trump. I've spent the last twenty-five years around famous people and most are not at all like that. Most people get to a certain point of notoriety where they think, being with me is inherently entertainment enough. Wrong! *I was president, you can tell your friends you met me.* No, Trump isn't like that at all. In the TV business we say, 'he comes to play.' He's got something he's bringing over. He's working for you. It's usually a vulgar joke or some completely true observation about people, but always he has something interesting to say, and he has a deep joy in him and appetite for life! People like that enliven your world. So many others just take."

One arena in which Carlson believes Trump's odd collection of personal attributes gives him a real advantage is foreign policy.

"I meet people for a living," says Tucker, "it's my job. Put Trump up next to George W. Bush. Bush is just waiting for you to ask him some question about foreign policy so he can pretend to know something he doesn't really understand. Bush is an idiot posing as an erudite person. Trump will say things like, 'You know,

Xi is really tall.'" He laughs, continues channeling Trump on China's Communist Party. "*You see him review the Chinese military, they're all about five-foot-six, five-foot-eight. Xi is six foot. If you want to go through all of China, 1.3 billion people and trying to cast the guy who should be in charge, you would find Xi. He towers over the others, he's a giant.'*"Tucker pauses. "Trump is truly convinced that the point is significant, and I'm convinced, too. He's Han Chinese and he's six feet tall? How'd that happen?

"His analysis of world affairs starts with things like this. He said to me once: 'The Chinese are really afraid of the Japanese,' which is true, because the Japanese are like animals, like a trapped wombat, they'll just bite your face. I'm talking to Xi and Xi's going on about Japan — I mean, Japan is a little island, they don't even have an army. But Xi is very worried about Japan. Why wouldn't he be? They rolled into Manchuria and ate people, and the Chinese still remember that." And he's totally right. Like his analysis of Ukraine versus Russia. If you ask Trump, he'll tell you immediately from memory the manpower of the Russians versus the Ukrainian army, the landmass of Ukraine versus Russia, the energy deposits of Ukraine versus Russia and he'll be, like, *Who's going to win?* This is a completely asymmetrical contest and the bigger guy over time is going to win because he's got more lives to expend. Why has no one else said that? It's true, actually. That way of thinking allows him insights into American foreign policy that have been unsurpassed. No one has been more insightful about American foreign policy than Trump. And I do think foreign policy is a little easier because you're less in the weeds, you can take the bigger picture, which suits Trump's thinking in the first place. If you ask Trump what we're going to do about Social Security, that's a math problem. It's very complex. People have been tinkering with it for ninety years and it's not really clear what you do. But when you're talking about the great powers, you're using the broadest possible brush and that is Trump's area. He was the first one to ask, what's the point of NATO? And everyone called him an idiot. But if we go to war with Russia, won't they just go to China? And then you have the largest landmass teamed up with the largest population. Trump does have a genius that bypasses a lot of the detail, and it doesn't always serve him. You can't run the Department of Justice that way, but you can inform people's thinking in a really important way."

The strength of Tucker's bond with Trump was apparent on March 7, 2020, when he went to Mar-a-Lago to press his rising concerns about Covid-19 to the president personally. At the time almost all other conservative commentators were downplaying the threat of the virus — and their liberal counterparts, in a frenzy over the first Trump impeachment, were likewise giving it short shrift — but Tucker's sources were telling him that Beijing was lying, the devastation in China was massive, and what was coming here was going to be catastrophic.

"I told him," Carlson acknowledges now of his meeting with the president, "he could easily lose the election over Covid."

A couple of days later, he was sounding the warning in equally blunt terms to his audience. "People you trust, people you probably voted for, have spent weeks minimizing what is clearly a very serious problem," he said. "'It's just partisan politics,' they say. 'Calm down. In the end this was just like the flu and people die from that every year. Coronavirus will pass."

Such people, he continued, were "wrong," what was coming would be "major," and "It's definitely not just like the flu. . . . The

Chinese coronavirus will get worse; its effects will be far more disruptive than they are right now. That is not a guess; it is inevitable no matter what they're telling you. Let's hope everyone stops lying about that, and soon."

"I don't have any actual authority," he told *Vanity Fair*, after the news of his visit with Trump leaked to *The New York Times*, "I'm just a talk show host. But I felt — and my wife strongly felt — that I had a moral obligation to try and be helpful in whatever way possible."

It was probably the greatest public mistake he ever made, and it would not take him long to realize how devastatingly wrong he'd been, or to begin trying to repair the damage.

Over the ensuing couple of years, no one on the air would be more skeptical of the governing narrative on Covid-19, more fierce in condemning the lockdowns and vaccine mandates, or more welcoming of those doctors putting their careers on the line to challenge the government/Big Pharma line.

Indeed, just eighteen days after the Mar-a-Lago meeting, though still persuaded the pandemic would be severe, he was already starting to express skepticism about the official narrative, specifically regarding the government's suppression of potentially life-saving treatments. "Hydroxychloroquine is the ideal medicine," he said March 25, a drug, sneeringly dismissed by left as a result of what proved to be a bogus study. "If it turns out to be an effective treatment against coronavirus, things will change fast in this country and for the better. . . . Donald Trump is not the only person who thinks hydroxychloroquine might be effective. A lot of practicing physicians think so, too. Our leaders should be clear about that. And yet many of them are lying about it at a time when we are desperate for the truth. The thing we need, above all, is the truth."

Less than two weeks after that, on April 7, he was urging viewers to question *all* federal guidance on Covid, noting that in their alleged efforts to curb the pandemic, the authorities were moving to crush our most fundamental freedoms. "'*You can't go to church until we have a vaccine,*' he portrayed them as dictating. '*The truth is we have no choice.*' Heard that before? That's a familiar phrase in Washington. It ought to make you nervous. Do what I say, follow my orders without question or complaint or a million people will die. The oceans will rise. The polar bears will perish. The human race itself will go extinct."

After that, there was no turning back. "Not a single politician making these decisions has bothered to explain the science behind them," he intoned on April 20, "specifically which studies show that staying indoors at home — at the pharmacy, at the grocery store — is safer than being outdoors. Politicians don't tell us, and they're never asked. The media support these decisions reflexively."

A month after that, on May 22, he was challenging the very premise behind everything: that Covid-19 represented an existential threat to humanity. He noted that the World Health Organization had "estimated a case fatality rate of 3.4 percent. It's horrifying. It scared the hell out of the country. It scared the hell out of us. I think we repeated those numbers to you on this show. But they were totally wrong. We now know, thanks to widespread blood testing, that the virus isn't that deadly. An enormous percentage of coronavirus infections produce mild symptoms or no symptoms at all. They're asymptomatic. The death toll is a tiny fraction of what we were told it would be."

When the vaccine was rushed to market in early 2021, and widely celebrated as the ultimate game changer, Carlson was quick to challenge this new deadly falsehood, proclaiming the mRNA shots are a "dangerous and ineffective product at this point against Omicron," and advising that "no one should get them."

How, I ask, did he come to change his mind so decisively?

At the beginning, he says, "I assumed the CDC wouldn't lie. I was wrong. Then they kept the weed dispensaries open but closed the churches. Nobody I knew died from Covid. The only person I knew who did die, would die from the vax. So like most people, I was just kind of living it. And it was clear what they were telling us was a lie. It was supposed to kill everybody but it didn't. I kept waiting for people to die, like they said they would, and nobody did. Except one person I knew pretty well who took the vaccine and immediately had a heart attack. This was in January 2021, before doctors had been ordered to lie, and his doctor said the obvious, that it was the vax, his death was a vax reaction.

"Being a total skeptic anyway, really just watching it all unfold, and its being so completely different from what they claimed it was going to be, that was enough."

CHAPTER FIFTEEN

O dd as it might seem, Tucker Carlson does not own a television. He does not have one in either his Florida home or in his home in Maine. On an average day, the only time he so much as sees a TV screen is when he's looking at a guest on his studio monitor.

In this sense, Carlson might be regarded as a Luddite, the gently mocking term for those with an abiding distaste for technological progress.

Yet, unlike the late-eighteenth-century English weavers from whom the term is derived — who destroyed the new steam-powered looms that threatened their livelihoods — he doesn't so much hate the technology as the uses to which it's been put: the ways it's made us more soulless, and how it has served to undermine family and community.

One day he tells me that one of his children recently showed him an episode of the popular black-comedy HBO series *The White Lotus*, noting he couldn't even make it to the end.

"It just made me too sad. I thought, 'I don't want these horrible people in my life. Everyone's lying. They don't love each other. I want to be as far away from them as I can. It was worse than pornography, because it was so sophisticated in its execution. The episode I saw there were two married couples in fake marriages, fake for different reasons. Can you imagine not even trusting your spouse?" His eyes widen, in that classic Tucker expression of disbelief. ""We don't have any fake people in our world, at all. That's the most important thing, that the center of your life is real. That's your armor for when you go out in the world, and the place to be able to retreat back into where you can fully be yourself."

As we talk, Susie stands at the kitchen counter, hand-writing a letter to a friend. Susie is a big fan of handwriting. Tucker once made the mistake of buying her an iPad, thinking she'd get great use of the calendar function. She never even turned it on, and it went into a drawer.

Tucker very much admires this. "Our stationery bills are very high," he laughs. "She makes phone calls, she doesn't watch TV, she loves books, reads about two hours a day, she writes things out because the physical touch of writing means something to her; you think about people as you write with your hand. She really is like the last Japanese soldier in Okinawa. She's just living in another age. And she's way happier. You have a conversation with her, and she looks at you. Living with her, you see the cost of progress. She doesn't imagine that all change is an improvement. And it's so inspiring for me to see, because she's right."

How different would his own life be, he is asked, if he didn't have a smartphone?

"Oh, it would be wonderful! I'd probably just spend the whole day bullshitting with dudes in my kitchen, like now. But my wife actually lives that life."

He pauses. "Because really, an interior world, a personal life that's completely authentic and loving and protective, that's more important than anything else — your salary, your house, everything. Being focused on other people, rather than yourself, lacking self-consciousness — those are signs of emotional health. If you don't have that you become fearful, self-hating, and narcissistic, like a lot of people I know. Narcissism is actually self-hatred misidentified as self-love; narcissists hate themselves so much, they're so weak inside and so fearful of self-examination, they have to turn everything outward, away from themselves. Narcissism is like having a suppurating, throbbing wound that you can't bear to have touched because it hurts so much. That's why narcissists inevitably self-sabotage. You see this in the public sphere with leaders who are narcissistic: they always end up hurting themselves, and it's clearly intentional. And they don't even realize they're doing it. I've watched political figures, including some I know very well, hamstring themselves, create scandals when they're ascending — just when they're getting traction, becoming more popular — and all of a sudden, they'll say something that's so damaging."

He pauses a moment, thoughtful. "People hurt themselves a lot. I think that's what separates people from the animals. Animals don't commit suicide. Animals don't destroy themselves on purpose. People do. Politicians especially do, because they're the most insecure.

"You don't want any falseness or lying in your immediate world at all. That's more dangerous than cancer."

Neither Tucker nor Susie is on social media. In her case it is "because of the hate. He's a target for a lot of people, and I truly don't understand it except, I guess, people need somebody to attack or blame."

But Tucker, she says, genuinely doesn't care what people think, "he just doesn't worry about stuff like that. It's so refreshing, I wish I was more like that."

Susie's aversion to the news has everything to do with maintaining a level of inner peace. "I just don't want to be mad at people," as she puts it. "I don't want to feel angry. I don't like if people hate my husband, but I don't hate them. It's not that I feel sorry for them, because that sounds condescending. "On the other hand, even though I'm not on social media and don't watch TV, I do live in this century, and I talk to people and I'm not dumb. So we have security." She pauses. "One time we were in Logan airport and this woman shoved herself against Tucker and swore at him, 'Go to hell, you eff-er!' I can't believe people talk like that. But they know where you live, and it can be concerning sometimes."

What's startling is that Susie has never seen Tucker's show, save for one time she visited the studio to watch in person. But she does read his monologues every day just before they're sent off to the producers.

Moreover, she's long had a recurring alarm set on her phone for every night at 7:55 p.m. That's when she texts him to tell him that he is "the best husband in the world." (I asked Susie about this after I noticed, during the three nights in a row that I sat in studio, at precisely 7:55 Tucker picked up his phone, furrowed his brow playfully, and said under his breath, "Really? The best? How does she know that?").

"I do it because I'm so proud of him, and I'm thinking of him, and I want him to know that he's loved. He's great and that's a big job.

I can't believe he's going live on TV for an hour and I'm, like, sitting at dinner with a friend," she tells me later on.

I ask why she thinks her husband is such a target, even more so than other current and former Fox News personalities. "I think he's a threat. I think he says what he thinks is true. Why doesn't Sean Hannity get this sort of reaction? I don't watch his show, so I don't really know what he thinks, but it's my understanding Tucker speaks about topics that are more, I guess, controversial. He believes that the whole thing with Ukraine and the war and that the Ukrainian government is anti-Christian. He's not afraid to say that, and I don't know why other people can't speak to that. Then the whole Covid thing — he was never afraid to say people should have a choice in what they want to put in their bodies. Like, why not? He's not a follower. Maybe that's why people hate him, because he won't follow. That does kind of make me sad that people think that you all have to look the same, think the same. He's always going to be honest with himself."

Tucker's father, in contrast, watches Tucker's show every night, and Susie's mother not only does the same but texts Tucker during commercial breaks, and he always responds immediately. She has health issues and limited mobility, Susie says, so "it's a gift for her to have that special connection every night."

Having Tucker Carlson as a father has not always been easy for their four children, now all in their twenties, Susie admits, adding with a smile "We have a strict no-Googling-pop rule in this house." Then, more seriously: "The toughest thing in his life has been the kids struggling with his job. That your job, or your persona, has a negative impact on your own child is really hard, and he has real guilt over that. I don't think they'll ever understand it until they're parents themselves.

But I feel like he feels he's doing what God called him to do. He's been given these gifts and he's so articulate, and he feels like he makes a difference.

"We have conversations with them, and the conversations can be difficult because they don't want to feel like they're criticizing him. On the other hand, they want to know we understand that it's not easy for them. Which we do. But the dynamic between a parent and a child is that the child never really feels fully heard. I know we try our best, but it kills me they have to worry about if their friends are their friends because they like them, or because they found out who their dad was. Or, that someone won't be friends with them because they don't like who their dad is. It's super hard for one of my girls to go in public with him because she's very shy and doesn't like attention. And she doesn't like to feel like people are looking at her, which they do. If you go to a restaurant, you can focus on the table, but you can tell people are talking about him and pointing, and then people ask if they can get their picture taken. That's not a happy thing for her. So now, when she comes home, we just don't go out for dinner." She pauses, smiles again. "Except I'm a terrible cook, so when she's home we get a lot of takeout."

Tucker, for his part, takes a far more traditional approach in raising his own children than he experienced with his own father. "I have three daughters; that's a huge part of it. And things are so different now anyway. And the biggest difference is I live with their mother. If you've got one parent, you're all in on that parent. My dad was extraordinary, and I knew that, but he was not conventional, which can be hard. I tried to be more sensitive to that with my own children. Like, don't be *too* out of step, or *too fuck the world* — not even when I feel that way."

CHAPTER
SIXTEEN

Among the many things that set Carlson apart from others on TV who, superficially, do more or less the same thing, is that he is far more interested in the condition of the culture than in standard ideological combat. Indeed, those interests extend beyond today's "culture wars," vital as are the moral issues at their heart, to the basic questions of the nature of the environment — physical, spiritual, and emotional — which is essential to the nourishment of the human soul. This regularly leads him into deeply felt disquisitions on nature, the arts, and architecture, statements that between the lines reveal the breadth of his knowledge, as well as the serious thought he's given to the role such things play in a flourishing society.

Unsurprisingly, this can be somewhat confusing to those, including potentates within the Republican Party, whose own deep thinking tends to be limited to economic and other more obviously pragmatic concerns.

Carlson takes a view both longer term and deeper. "I look at the country and I notice that virtually everything built after 1945 is less attractive, less pleasing, less human-centered than everything built before," as he put it to a Des Moines, Iowa, audience in 2022. "Think about your own town. The prettiest buildings, they're built in 1920. The closer you get to our current moment, the more everything looks like a Dollar Store, and the Republican Party somehow found itself in this position where they feel like they have to defend the aesthetics of the Dollar Store and the economics of it. It's an atrocity that diminishes people, that destroys God's creation, that oppresses us with its ugliness. That is true, and no one wants to say it because, I don't know, some libertarian think-tank was paid to tell you that the Dollar Store is attractive? I don't think it is, actually. Their idea of beauty is a female impersonator screaming at you. No. Beauty is nature. . . . The Republican Party should be for nature and not just in its aesthetics. Not just in its design, but in its human relationships. People are born wanting certain things."

"It really matters," Carlson picks up the theme one night after the broadcast. "If you live in an environment that's disposable, it really has an effect on you."

He points to his living-room walls, of whitewashed pine shiplap. "Wood is no more expensive than drywall — I mean, sure, it varies by kind. But in general, to clad your wall in wood on studs, versus taping drywall, is not more expensive. And then you're surrounded, in the rooms you live, eat, and sleep in, by a living thing. That affects you a lot. Sleep in a room that has wood walls, which I do exclusively, then sleep in a room that's clad in white fucking plasterboard and tell me how you feel in the morning."

I mention that I have plaster walls in the building where I live in New York, noting it was built in 1917. Tucker nods meaningfully. "That's a world of difference. You know what's in that plaster? *Horsehair.* That's what adheres it. Next time you have anything done to your plaster, look at it — the binder will literally be hair from horses. So, you do have a living thing in your walls. And you can feel it. Acoustically it makes a difference, too."

Carlson's guiding insight is that such things are the opposite of incidental and trivial, that it is precisely such details that define societies in their entirety and guarantee the well-being of their citizens.

"Here's how we know if the ideology is a good one," as he put it in the Iowa speech.

"Noble ideologies produce beautiful results. They produce beauty. Poisonous ideologies produce ugliness. There's a reason the architecture in Bulgaria in 1975 was hideous — because Sofia in 1975 was controlled by the Soviet Union. Soviet architecture was horrifying, so was architecture under Mao. They knocked down everything worth having been built during the preceding millennia, and they replaced it with concrete boxes. Why'd they do that? Because those boxes, those buildings, that architecture, that design sent a very clear message — which is you are worth nothing. There's no beauty for you. Now why is beauty so important, and why did tyrants always destroy it? They destroy it because beauty reminds you that the most important things are eternal. They're unchanging. beauty is recognizable across cultures, across centuries.

"Why does beauty happen? Because it's derived from nature. It's derived from God's creation. The closer we are to God's creation, the straighter the path and the better the path."

"I've always loved trees," he tells me another evening, "they're alive. They have intent. Especially conifers. If it's conifer versus deciduous, put me strongly on the conifer side. The eastern white pine is the mack daddy badass of the forest, everything about it is dignified and useful. It's just an incredible tree that has greatly enhanced human civilization and human joy."

Since this is one of his go-to subjects, he speaks with absolute joy. "Did you know eastern pines were the leading source of masts for the British Navy? The Brits controlled everything from Hong Kong to the Bahamas and they did it thanks to their navy, and their navy did it with masts from eastern white pines. But they are also remarkable on their own terms. If you walk through a forest in western Maine, it's a mix of birch, maple, oak, spruce, hemlock — which are lesser trees in my opinion — fir and pines. Our red pines are fine, we have a lot of them, but compared to the eastern white pine, it's a weak tree. It's not majestic, it's not dominant. But if you're in the forest, and you come to a place where sunlight is coming through, you'll know there's a white pine there, because all the other trees are like, *Wow, we gotta give this guy some space.* They back the fuck off. Just an amazing tree, one of the wonders of nature."

That Carlson so regularly, unprompted, goes into reveries about nature and its vital role in human well-being makes his ideological foes' charge that he is "anti-environment" more than a little odd. Then, again, unlike them he is careful to make the distinction between that which humankind can and cannot control.

"I'm a complete environmental crazy person on the actual environment," he tells me the next morning. "What frustrates me is that the concern about climate is inverse to the concern about the actual environment."

Carlson — who personally never wears deodorant or socks — nods toward the beach beyond his Florida home. A red tide has killed off millions of tons of sea life, and dead fish carpet the beach, their scales of iridescent pinks, purples, and blues glistening in the sun; others are hard, flat, crusted, and brown, with swim bladders protruding from their mouths like dirty, inflated condoms. The algae blooms that make the beaches inaccessible and the air difficult to breathe are not part of the natural cycle, they are the result of agricultural, developmental, and sewage runoff.

"It's not about the temperature," Carlson says, "it's about us dumping a bunch of shit into the water. If everyone within a hundred miles of here was driving a Tesla it wouldn't fix the red tide. It's completely a blame shift. You're putting crap, human feces, in the water, and that's something we could really do something about."

Eight hours later, in the studio, the spectators for this evening's show happen to be a pair of local fishermen, both middle-aged in blue jeans, tucked flannel shirts, and low-slung baseball hats. During a commercial break, Carlson asks them about the red tide. He's thinking of doing a segment on the subject but is unsure how such a complicated issue can fit into a four-and-a-half minute cable-news block.

As so often proves to be the case, the ordinary citizens have greater insight than the alleged experts. "There's three pieces to the pie," volunteers one, "phosphate mining, agricultural interests like sugar, and coastal development. And how we change will be through education, which will bring the noise to cause a shift in political will."

Carlson gives the man his phone number. Two nights later, a red-tide segment runs on *Tucker Carlson Tonight* with a guest recommended by the fisherman.

The subject of living in harmony with the natural world is never far from Tucker's mind, and that evening, back in his kitchen, he is on it again.

"Why would someone ever plant an oak tree?" he asks. "It takes eighty years to become concave, they're never going to see it; it will still be this ugly little sapling when they die. It's because someday it will be this majestic thing that people they never knew will love and enjoy." He pauses. "Really, all of human civilization is a testament to that impulse that people have to build things they won't personally benefit from. All of my spiritual beliefs are grounded in that — seeing people's kindness to each other, doing something to help others for no reason. Because in the end, I really do think most people are possessed by the desire to be kind."

CHAPTER
SEVENTEEN

The next day's monologue had its origins in a conversation Tucker had over dinner a few days ago with a friend he met in Iraq and his friend's girlfriend. Though the subject — mankind's feebleness in the face of elemental forces, and our desperation to control the uncontrollable — would seem more suited to a philosophical symposium than a political show on cable TV, it passionately engages Carlson.

"This woman I had dinner with the other night, everything about her past would make you sure you'd know how her life would wind up, right?" he tells me. "She was a meth addict, and raised in foster care, and got pregnant at seventeen. But it didn't wind up that way at all. She was smart, and put-together, and lovely. So, obviously, she made that happen. People are capable of remarkable things — and that's true of every single person.

"Then, again, maybe we have less agency than we think we do. Maybe, good and bad, we're not really in charge of all that much. We think we are but we're not. We are acting, but we're also being acted on. We think we control the world, but we're really living in an ant farm. And we didn't build the ant farm. There are exterior forces — unseen, exterior forces — that are completely real, that are acting on us at all times, for good or for bad, period. That is 100 percent true and totally real."

Tucker did not, as he says, "grow up super religious," and he acknowledges "I don't have theological language, which anyway I'm not interested in, because it's totally overused and meaningless. It's just dogs barking at this point; you don't even hear it. But I know for a fact there are forces outside us acting on us everywhere, every day. There's no rational explanation for it because it's not rational, it's supernatural.

"And our never-ending attempt to exert control, be it over the weather or our own mortality, always leads to the same predictable end. Because we are not in control."

In fact, Carlson finds that so many of his contemporaries are convinced otherwise to be nothing short of hilarious. "The idea that the only things that are real are the things we can see and measure and weigh on scales, that's idiotic. No culture before ours has ever thought that; I don't think we need more evidence than that that we're completely stupid. We imagine we have powers that we don't, that our knowledge is more complete than it is; we're just completely besotted with hubris and stupidity. Every other culture — from the fucking Aztecs, to the Babylonians, to medieval Europe — understands that, yes, there's a human sphere and we're making these little decisions — coffee or tea, whatever — and then there are the real decisions, like, when do I die? Or what's the weather?" He bursts out laughing. "The decisions that matter are not ours!

"There's no explanation from evolutionary biology that accounts for the overwhelming empathy when you really understand someone's struggles. Just as it's impossible to rationally explain the equally irrational desire that comes over all people at certain points to destroy, whether it's other people, or things, or themselves. What is that? Do you have some sort of advantage if you destroy yourself or the world around you? No, you have a massive disadvantage. So why is this inside of you? Because there is a force acting on you from outside, obviously! Evil spirits, good spirits, all this stuff we dismiss as untrue is all taken as a fact of life by every other culture in the world.

"And if you just take twenty minutes a day to sit in silence, you'll feel it. It's not hard."

I ask if that's a symptom of how we live these days, overstimulated and under-fulfilled, as likely to spend our days with technology than with other human beings and our natural surroundings?

He nods his agreement. "Completely true! The society we've built is inconsistent with our fundamental, unchanging nature. "We never experience nature. People don't see the stars. Humanity's spent millions of years having night and day determined by sunlight, and all of a sudden it's not. Thomas Edison said, 'I'm flipping a switch and suddenly nature doesn't matter.' I don't think anxiety attacks were a thing in the neolithic period! People didn't wake up in spiritual crisis asking, *Why am I here?* — I think the quest for protein provided enough meaning.

"We are way too isolated from each other, and from basic parts of ourselves. The cruelest punishment we administer in our society is solitary confinement — that's all you need to know. I miss living in a society that recognizes that obvious truth. And it's not enough to just blame Pfizer, which I'm happy to do for almost every crime, but I think the problem is deeper than Pfizer. It's us."

CHAPTER
EIGHTEEN

T ucker regularly makes clear he despises nothing more than ass-kissing, in the professional realm and otherwise. "I don't come from a flattery culture," he says. "Among the people I work with, there's affection and loyalty and love in abundance, but no flattery whatsoever. You can't trust people who act that way; someone who kisses ass doesn't respect himself, and someone who doesn't respect himself is a dangerous person. If you're dealing with a boot-licker, what you're seeing is not what's in that person's heart."

He pauses before expanding on the thought. "Also, it blows up the idea of egalitarianism — that we're all created equal — not in ability, but in moral value — and should act that way. It's why there's so much ass-kissing under socialism, because they don't believe that."

When approached in public by groupies or autograph seekers, he's gracious, though can also be a bit standoffish.

But it's an entirely different story if a stranger is interested in seriously engaging with him. Indeed, while he hasn't read *The New*

York Times or *Washington Post* in years, and gets no news from television or the internet, those he meets in the course of daily life have been a veritable fount of source material for his show. His phone buzzes around the clock with texts from an army of characters, many suggesting topics to be aired.

"Tucker gives his phone number to nearly everyone he meets," says Wells, "everywhere he travels. Southwest Airlines flight attendants, waiters, anyone. It can drive me crazy, but he gets amazing stories that way and it improves the show greatly. Some of them are bogus, of course, but the team can figure that out pretty quickly."

Carlson estimates he's in regular communication with roughly four hundred everyday people who text him links, one-liners, local news items. I spoke to nurses, commercial-airline pilots, real-estate agents, and actors, each of whom had had a random encounter with Carlson that ended in Tucker giving them his personal cell-phone number. Some text him almost daily, and he always responds. Many admit to texting him even during his live broadcasts, and often he'll respond to these during commercial breaks. At one point, after we've been talking about an hour, Tucker checks and sees he has received 182 text messages.

Wilson, a blue-collar, thirty-nine-year-old father of three in suburban Atlanta, is one of those people. One time he sent Carlson a tweet from economist and *New York Times* columnist Paul Krugman that read, "Is there any good reason to believe that inflation hits low-income households especially hard?"

"Holy shit," Carlson shot back in response, and featured the tweet during the A block of that night's show.

"I'm just some normal guy," Wilson tells me, "but I was like, hell yeah, I just got to poke that idiot!"

Wilson — who asked I use a pseudonym lest progressives might attack his construction business — has also gotten advice from Tucker on personal issues, having in his youth had a drinking problem, and having been arrested several times. Now he wants to start a family.

"It was some of the best advice I've ever gotten, way longer than my email to him. And now I see him as a mentor on marriage problems, friend problems, work problems." When Wilson was in Washington, D.C., for work, Carlson invited him to watch a broadcast of the show. Today, they text daily and have dinner together about once a year, and Tucker has even gotten him into fly fishing. "He's a bigger part of my life than I am of his, obviously, because he's super famous, but he's a great guy who has shaped a lot of who I am today."

Michelle, a waitress from Big Sur, California — she also asked I use an assumed name — met the Carlsons when she waited on them one evening at the ritzy restaurant where she works. Since the place caters to a celebrity clientele, fame leaves her unimpressed. She's served Taylor Swift ("She just sat there in her stupid little sparkly sweater looking insecure"); Tom Hanks ("Just the freaking smugness"); and Kanye West in his Kim Kardashian phase ("No vibe to them at all, they look like little hobbits"). The evening the Carlsons walked in was just a week after Antifa's attack on their D.C. home, and as they got up to leave, Michelle felt compelled to break decorum. "'I'm very, very sorry about what happened last week,'" she said. "'This is disgusting and you don't deserve that behavior.'"

She then mentioned to Tucker that she appreciated his reporting on UFOs — the topic was a staple and audience favorite on his show — "and he got very excited and goes, 'You know, they're real.' And I said, 'Yes, yes I do,'" The two started discussing books on the subject, and have been in close communication ever since.

"I never, in a million years, used to consider myself conservative, or right-leaning," she allows. "I'm from California, born and raised." But since then she's sent Carlson interviews with doctors challenging Covid-19 dogma and stories about bizarre practices in California's voting procedures, both of which he used on the show. In 2021, during a surge in ISIS activity in Afghanistan, dubbed "ISIS-K" by the Biden administration, Michelle texted Carlson, "ISIS-K? Sounds like a cosmetics line." Carlson immediately asked if he could use it, which he did the following night.

"I was shocked when he started texting me back," Mike, a street cop in Washington, D.C., — also not his real name — tells me, but by now they've developed a regular back-and-forth. Just the previous night, after working a shooting in Washington's trendy Dupont Circle neighborhood that left two people dead, he contacted Carlson, detailing what local news reports were getting wrong.

"Command staff officials aren't going to talk to Tucker Carlson," he says; "the top level of any police department in every liberal big city in America are just going to toe the party line and hand out the b.s. talking points."

While working on a documentary about crime in Chicago for his *Tucker Carlson Originals* series on Fox Nation, Carlson phoned Mike for perspective on big-city policing. "We talked for a good, long time and he did very little talking." "'You've got a horrible, dangerous job,'" Tucker told him at the end of the call, "'thank you for being out there for us.' I was, like, 'Dude, thank *you*. I'm just a guy with a job, thank you for having a voice for little guys like me.'"

Of course, recognizable as he is, Tucker occasionally has less-than-pleasant public interactions with strangers. During these, he told a sympathetic podcaster, he finds himself "at a huge disadvantage . . . because everybody now has a video recorder on their phone." Moreover, he admits, it doesn't help that he can be "a serious dick," a tendency that at some moments he must try to "keep under control, since it's unattractive and doesn't achieve anything. . . . I'm not afraid of confrontation, obviously. But then you don't really want to be on video, being your ugliest self. You can be nice to fifty people, but if they get you just once on that. . ."

He goes on to describe an incident not long before when, at a restaurant with his fishing guide and his son, a woman at the adjacent table started baiting him, loudly referring to him as a sexist. "They're sitting right behind me, and so I whipped around and said 'Settle down, honey,'" and he was about to say more when his friend indicated they were taking video. "I don't have great eyesight at a distance in the dark because I'm fifty-three," but "they have a video camera, they're videotaping it. So I just sit there and just eat it. Yeah, and that's the better way, for sure. You shouldn't assault people in restaurants. The idea of confronting someone in public is so far out of anything I would ever do. I don't care who it is. If Satan was at the next booth in a restaurant, I wouldn't say word one. Because Satan gets to eat too, know what I mean?"

CHAPTER
NINETEEN

The podcast on which Tucker described the confrontation in the restaurant is called *Full Send*, and though it has two million subscribers on YouTube, as well as millions more across iTunes and Spotify, it's a safe bet that only a relative handful of Fox viewers — median age sixty-five — have ever heard of it. Its audience is overwhelmingly young men — specifically, given the content and tone of the broadcast, young men unembarrassed about *being* young men. This is a demographic that in recent decades has been increasingly derided by mainstream culture as afflicted by something called "toxic masculinity."

It is also a segment of the population Tucker very much wants to reach, and with whom he connects in a visceral way.

For among the things that most disturbs him about Western culture's drift toward the abyss is the relentless assault on traditional manhood. He recognizes, and will go on at length about, the vast, catastrophic consequences of the society's wholesale surrender to such folly. How, from the earliest age, boys today are told they are fundamentally flawed, and that their most natural impulses are misguided and illicit.

Tucker tells me that his message to young men is simple: "Act on your instincts, They're always right. Don't let them degrade you."

In this last, he is of course referring to embittered feminists, whose revolution has resulted in notions once given a hearing only in loony bins and at American universities now being taken as gospel everywhere America's elites hold sway and is reinforced daily as much on ESPN as it is in elementary school classrooms and the arts pages of *The New York Times*. Chief among these is that differences between the sexes in behavior, thought, and inclination are not healthy and normal functions of biology, but instead a matter of social conditioning.

So when young males do the sorts of things they always have — push back against dumb rules, crack wise, roughhouse, and, yes, assess those of the opposite sex based on looks — they are to be called on it and straightened out. Girls who parade in "Girl Power" T-shirts are to be celebrated as brave and forward-looking while any ten-year-old boy lunatic enough to show up at school in a "Boy Power" shirt, (if one could even be found), is a threat to be dispatched to the principal's office or psychiatric care for moral rehabilitation. When women struggle with the STEM — Science, Technology, Engineering, Math — subject it is the product of sexism, and allowances must be made; when men are indifferent to the works of Alice Walker, it is because they are callous and blind to beauty, and also probably racist.

The result of two generations of this is that young men are in crisis. They start school at five already 14 percent less school-ready than girls, and steadily lose ground from there. By now two million more women than men graduate from college every year, and even such formerly male-dominated professions as law and medicine now draw significantly more women than men; meanwhile, men with high-school degrees or less, especially aged twenty-five to thirty-four, face ever-rising rates of unemployment.

Little wonder that American young men are depressed and disheartened, with their rates of suicide and drug overdoses running four times those of women.

Tucker has shed much needed light on all of it, as well as another aspect of the problem arguably even more alarming: a precipitous decline in male potency attributable both to the psychological onslaught men have endured and contaminants in the nation's food supply. As Tucker spelled it out in a documentary on Fox Nation straightforwardly titled *The End of Men*, the suppression of men threatens the very survival of the species. The documentary examines the crisis in its various aspects, but its overriding message is that the sissified, feminized culture we've created — one in which even the military embraces wokeism in all its insanity — is a prescription for societal collapse. "Hard times make strong men," as the program has it, "weak men make hard times."

"Author C.S. Lewis warned of the West one day it would be filled with what he called 'men without chests,'" intones Tucker in the introduction, "and we see that prophecy coming true today. We call them, less poetically, man boobs. They're a physical manifestation of something bigger, the decline of manhood, of virility, of physical health, altogether which threaten to doom our civilization."

Leftist outlets predictably sneered. *The Nation*'s Joan Walsh described *The End of Men* as being "all about Carlson's white male panic and fear of being a 'weak man.'" Stephen Colbert called it "a celebration of homoeroticism;" MSNBC's Joy Reid said it was "blatant fascist postering."

But there is a good reason that Neilson rated *Tucker Carlson Tonight* the top show among even young Democrats. Like only a handful of others — Jordan Peterson, Joe Rogan, the irreverent gang at Barstool Sports — Tucker speaks to young men as do few others, with a directness and humor reflecting his own appreciation of what it means to be a man, even as he addresses their concerns and apprehensions.

The New York Times's quasi-conservative columnist Ross Douthat, of all people, got it exactly right in a piece the week Fox sent Tucker packing, when he noted that the "newer (and especially, younger) right, is defined by a politics of suspicion — a deep distrust of all institutions; a comfort with outsider forms of knowledge and conspiratorial theories; a hostility toward official mouthpieces and corporate-governmental alliances; a skepticism about American empire and a pessimism about the American future — that used to be much more the province of the left. . . . For any idea with an establishment imprimatur, absolute suspicion; for any outsider or skeptic, sympathy and trust. . . . Alienated from many more American institutions than their predecessors, staring at a record of elite failure and a social landscape where it seems like there's little to conserve, they increasingly start out where Carlson ended up — in a posture of reflexive distrust, where if an important American institution takes a position, the place to be is probably on the other side. . . . Which is why Carlson, more than other cable-news hosts, found a younger audience to supplement the baby boomer foundation that (for now) keeps the Fox News enterprise in business, putting the very old in touch with the very online."

Moreover, and hardly least, Carlson is always ready to mock the self-regard of prevailing left-wing culture. Himself a wise guy with an antic sense of the absurd, he connects naturally with guys twenty and thirty years younger. Who can doubt that many of them found it as hilarious as he did that among the charges lodged by Abby Grossberg in her "toxic workplace" brief against Tucker was that in his office was a poster of Nancy Pelosi in a swimsuit, and that a male colleague had suggested turning a breastfeeding room in Fox headquarters into a testicle-tanning studio.

This is the Tucker that the hosts of *Full Send*, a pair of twentysomething Canadians named Kyle Forgeard and Steiny, were delighted to have on their show. And, sure enough, their guest was soon riffing on Canada to make a deadly serious point about the decline of the West. Canadian "dudes," he observed good-naturedly, "have been emasculated by feminist theory," and our neighbor to the north obviously "needs an intervention — a loving but angry dad . . . to go to a coffee shop in downtown Toronto, and say to the men there 'Cut off your little ponytail, shave and be a man . . . '"

Canada was cursed, he added, "with this weird crossdressing prime minister" and "they've given up the will to live. They're, like, *I guess I should commit suicide now because my healthcare costs are too high*. No, the will to live is intimately connected with the sex drive, the will to create, to reproduce, to continue the species, to tell the world: *I am here. I matter*. That's the essential force in the universe and if that dies in a culture people become bitches. . . . The whole country has fallen under the spell . . . you wouldn't need an army to take over Canada; you just need a megaphone and some pillows, and you'd beat him in a pillow fight– — and just be, like: *No, dad's home. Knock it off*. If you did that for three days in downtown Ottawa, the whole country would be, like: *Oh my God, I can't believe that we were under this spell where we thought our whole purpose in life was to buy shit on Amazon and then kill ourselves. . . .* This is happening in the States, too. I'm not just singling out Canada. It's happening all over the West, in every English-speaking country. Australia and New Zealand were real countries five years ago. They're not anymore, the people have been broken. Their spirit has been broken. . . . Where's the Australian spirit, like, wrestling alligators? Isn't this a country of ex-cons? It was a penal colony. Where's their spirit? Well, it's gone. It's totally broken."

The *Full Send* hosts asked Carlson about Andrew Tate, a thirty-six-year-old internet personality and former kickboxer, who is a media paragon of toxic masculinity run amuck. Tate unembarrassedly calls himself a misogynist, and at the time was being held in Romania on apparently trumped-up charges of sex trafficking; young women who'd worked for him as cam girls having alleged they'd been abused and psychologically coerced by Tate.

This is the sort of topic others in the media shy away from. But Tucker has covered the case closely on his show and finds Tate a figure of genuine interest.

"First of all," he says, "he's really smart. I'm almost fifty-four, so I'm really old. There are parts of what he says that are so far out of my world or context or experience. I'm going to be honest, there's some that I miss about Andrew Tate. But the spirit that animates Andrew Tate is very clear and obvious and it's not a malicious spirit, at all. Andrew Tate's core message is: respect yourself; act like you're worth something; achieve something; do something; get the fuck off the couch; put down the porn; go do something with your life. You're given this amazing thing, your life, and what are you going to do with it? I feel like that's the greatest message that anyone could give. It just tells you everything about the people in charge that that's threatening. How is that threatening? That's self-improvement. You may not agree with or understand some things that Tate says, which is where I am, but that's not the point. The point is: underneath it all, what is he saying? He's saying respect yourself; you are worthy of respect. Live in a way where others will respect you. That is the most needed message anyone can hear. . . . The most interesting thing about Andrew Tate is not Andrew Tate. It's the reaction to Andrew Tate. I have a son. If someone told my son to respect yourself, be worthy of respect, get up early, exercise, achieve something, I'd be like, thank you. That's the message I give my son anyway because I'm a father. Why would that be threatening? Because you don't want an independent self-respecting population in your country. That's why. And, so, they're, like, *oh, Andrew Tate's a sexual harasser.* The same people who were on pedo island with Epstein, the same people were friends with Harvey Weinstein."

Who, exactly, are "they," one of the hosts asks.

"From what I can tell, on the basis of my limited knowledge, this is a conspiracy of like-minded instincts. It's not that every douchebag in the world has a conference call every morning to decide how we can suppress the human spirit. But all of them have the same reaction to Andrew Tate. He's speaking to young men and he's telling them stop being passive, to do something impressive with your life. To act — not to overthrow the government, but just be a man. That is so threatening to them. I'm talking about the media and heads of state, which are the two main players in this ongoing effort to suppress and degrade and to kill the spirit of the population. They act effectively as one. There's very clearly coordination among different elements of this group, the people who are benefiting from the way our society — not just in the United States or Canada but throughout the West — is organized; the people who are the beneficiaries of that are the people with bullshit jobs working at NBC News or some stupid nonprofit, like the Atlantic Council, all those people whose jobs are effectively unjustifiable. What are you doing exactly to make this a better, freer, more prosperous society? They have no answer because they're not doing anything. They're doing the opposite. All of those people see Andrew Tate and think: *that guy has to shut up.*"

Late in the interview, one of the *Full Send* guys asks Tucker about his greatest regret.

First, he says, obviously, was defending the Iraq War. And he also has "a million regrets about not being more skeptical, calling people names when I should have listened to what they were saying. Look, when you, when someone makes a claim, there's only one question that's important at the very beginning, which is is the claim true or not?... And for too long, I participated in the culture where I was like, anyone who thinks outside these pre-prescribed lanes, is crazy, is a conspiracy theorist. And I just really regret that, and I'm ashamed that I did that."

Still, he adds, "partly it was age and partly was the world that I grew up in. So when you look at me, and you're like, 'Yeah, of course, they're a part of the means of control.' — that's obvious to you, because you're twenty-eight. But I just didn't see it at all, at all. And I'm ashamed."

CHAPTER
TWENTY

Like almost everyone else, in recent years Tucker Carlson has lost friendships over politics. Surely the most painful such loss was his falling out with his old mentor P.J. O'Rourke following Donald Trump's election to the presidency. A confirmed NeverTrumper, the iconic satirist regarded Trump as "unstable and dangerous."

Since their chance meeting in Nicaragua decades ago, the two had remained close. "P.J. O'Rourke was absolutely a hero of mine," says Tucker. "He loved spaniels, bird hunting, and northern New England. Those are some of the three great passions in my life; they aren't just hobbies, they are at the core of my life. My ideology, whatever that is, is bound up in that, and if you share that with somebody — if you appreciate the White Mountains in the fall, chasing woodcock with your Springer or your Brittany, we'll probably be friends.

"We had that and much more, and I loved P.J. Unfortunately, toward the end, you know, the Trump thing just divided people on every level and he was on the other side from me. But it didn't diminish my love for him and his wife."

Nor was the split of his doing. Tucker places a serious premium on friendship — almost as great as he places on family — and he regards the current mania for severing lifelong bonds over political difference with alarm and deep sadness.

"I have had a lot of relationships with liberals — I've been in journalism my whole life, most of the people I've dealt with were liberal — and I've never ended a relationship over politics. I never would, because I don't think it's the most important thing.

"I don't go on social media too often, but occasionally I'll hear so-and-so has been attacking me, and I'm surprised. *Really?* That person was my editor and my friend, we used to have dinner all the time. So I've definitely had liberals I really like stop talking to me, and it's always a little bit shocking.

"I have a religion, I don't need a new one. But for a lot of people on the left, it is their religion and this is a holy war, and they can't be friends with unbelievers."

This is hardly to suggest that he himself holds back in his attacks on doctrinaire progressives — this is Tucker Carlson we're talking about. No one more despises what the left stands for or regards with greater horror the damage done by its adherents. But except when using his platform to hit back at the most publicly vituperative figures on the other side, his contempt is in the abstract, not personal.

Of course, when he does return fire, he doesn't hold back.

In the aftermath of his firing, Fox released a slew of behind-the-scenes emails, blog posts, and off-the-record transcripts featuring Carlson at his most free-spoken; the higher-ups at the network apparently supposing these would soften him up for the settlement of his contract by casting him in a negative light. What was odd about this is that, while the things he's revealed to have said surely offend *New York Times* readers, whose every opinion and thought runs through a PC filter, they show exactly why Carlson is cherished by his audience. In a time of pussyfooting evasions, he speaks truths that almost no one else will, and does so in interesting, original, and, yes, often highly provocative ways.

Take, most notably, the Carlson missive to a Fox producer breathlessly reproduced by the *Times* in a piece headlined "Carlson's Text That Alarmed Fox Leaders." "A couple of weeks ago," it read, "I was watching video of people fighting on the street in Washington. A group of Trump guys surrounded an Antifa kid and started pounding the living shit out of him. It was three against one, at least. Jumping a guy like that is dishonorable obviously. It's not how white men fight. Yet suddenly I found myself rooting for the mob against the man, hoping they'd hit him harder, kill him. I really wanted them to hurt the kid. I could taste it. Then somewhere deep in my brain, an alarm went off: this isn't good for me. I'm becoming something I don't want to be. The Antifa creep is a human being. Much as I despise what he says and does, much as I'm sure I'd hate him personally if I knew him, I shouldn't gloat over his suffering. I should be bothered by it. I should remember that somewhere somebody probably loves this kid, and would be crushed if he was killed. If I don't care about those things, if I reduce people to their politics, how am I better than he is?"

The message *The New York Times* knew its readers would take was: Aha, proof (as if any were needed, in their minds) that Tucker

Carlson is a vicious racist. It couldn't be clearer in the only line that matters: "It's not how *white men* fight."

But the message just as clearly drawn by those familiar with Tucker is the one he intended: loathsome as our enemies are, and tempting as it is to descend to their level, we must expect better of ourselves.

"Fox told *The New York Times* they pulled me off because I was racist," as Tucker later tells me. "But I'm not racist, actually. I'm not insecure about that. If I was racist, I'd just say so. But I'm not. Being racist is not a crime — maybe a moral crime, but not a statutory crime — so if I was racist, I would just say so. What I said is that's not how white men fight, which as far as I'm concerned is true. I am a white man. I'm the son of a white man. I'm the grandson of a white man. So, if anyone's qualified to speak on the subject, it would be me. And that's not how white men fight is what I was raised to believe. In the culture I grew up in, you're not allowed to fight that way. I believe that, and I'm not embarrassed of that at all. But that was somehow translated to, I'm evil or I'm a racist or something."

Indeed, if anything, his straightforwardness on the subject — his openly wrestling with his contradictory feelings — surely made most longtime Tucker watchers appreciate him even more.

Where it's hard to imagine an Alexandria Ocasio-Cortez or Joe Scarborough or Stephen Cobert capable of such reflection and self-knowledge, let alone an Antifa or Black Lives Matter militant, in Carlson's case it came as a matter of course, even in a private communication.

As one online Tucker admirer knowingly reacted to the supposedly damning text: "Carlson is right — it isn't how white men in the

US are raised — to gang up in a fist fight against a single individual. It is a hard core principle we learned on the playgrounds growing up that if you have a disagreement that requires a physical fight, you do it one on one, and friends and family stay out of it. I was on both sides of this more than once growing up — fighting and enforcing the one on one rule. I imagine any white guy my age was on both sides or observed being applied. . . . Carlson's detractors think this text message will make him look bad. I disagree — I think most people will read it and think that if that was why he was fired, it was unjust."

More, in their misbegotten war on Tucker's reputation, the geniuses at Fox also failed to grasp that the words he marshals in his ongoing war on political correctness, shocking as they sometimes register to the Carlson-untrained ear, are themselves part of his message. If his language is provocative, sometimes even transgressive, he means it to be; but he is interested in clarity and does not aim to mislead.

"They tried to tell *The New York Times* and everybody else they took me off because I was commenting on some video I saw," Tucker tells me, "when what I was actually doing was counseling one of my producers to not let politics define other people. Because it's unhealthy. It's un-Christian. It's wrong."

If Tucker is disturbed by how the world has been sundered by politics, he is especially troubled by the depth of the divide it has created within so many families. "It's evil," he says flatly, "evil by definition to divide children from their parents, which is what wokeness does by intention. And awful as we know it is, I think too many people still don't take it seriously enough. In the world I live in, affluent, educated people send their kids to these schools where the chances they'll be destroyed and separated from their family is very high. But the residual prestige of these schools gets parents to buy into it.

"I can't imagine anything worse than losing contact with a child over politics. I don't care what politics my kids have, who they're having sex with, or what they believe — I would never disown my own children, ever, for any reason, and I think most parents feel that way. But the separation comes from the kids, the kids disowning their parents, and it's a terrifying thing."

For a man assumed by his adversaries to be ideologically driven and callous, it's striking how often Carlson talks about the importance of nurturing personal relationships. Speaking at the Heritage Foundation, he cautioned the well-heeled crowd to hold on to their classic books, because the digital versions were being undermined by the woke, then added "don't throw away your relationships with other people, because they can't be disappeared, either. The material, the physical things that you can smell, those are the things that you can trust — your spouse, your dogs, your children, especially your dogs, but you know, your actual friendships, your college roommates, people in person. . . . I think the only way to stay sane is to cling more tightly to the things that you can smell. And I've really gotten to the point where if I can't smell it, I'm not dealing with it."

When the axe fell, Tucker was seriously moved by the outpouring of support from strangers, and of course his close friends rallied to his side. But what touched him as much as anything was hearing from Bill Press, one of his old liberal counterparts on *Crossfire*, who heard the news in France. "That meant a lot," says Carlson simply.

"Bill's eighty-two, and you'd never know it — the hardest-working man I've ever known. Just a wonderful guy."

P.J. O'Rourke passed away in February, 2022, and Carlson is grateful that by then they'd begun to heal the rift.

"I had lunch with him before he died. I didn't know he was going to die. But we talked.

"PJ was a deep person, and all deep people are sad on some level. There's a lot to be sad about, if you let yourself experience it. He was fully connected to nature and the seasons, which if you're not, you're an idiot and missing something super important. You're missing wisdom."

The evening O'Rourke died Carlson's monologue was a eulogy for his friend. He was "one of the very few people in journalism," it concluded, "who cared about the right things. He loved his wife, his children, northern New England, his spaniels, bird hunting, having lunch with his friends, tobacco. He was a man in full — a great man."

CHAPTER
TWENTY-ONE

O ne morning over breakfast, the conversation turns to the close call Carlson experienced in 2001, when his plane almost crashed near Dubai.

I ask if he can describe what he was feeling at that moment.

"I was very upset," he replies evenly. "I definitely wasn't feeling the peace of certainty. Actually, I was filled with regret. It was like, Wow, I'm a shitty person. Not comforting at all."

The subject has come up unexpectedly, in relation to a topic his show had recently been covering: a string of logistical calamities in the airline industry that seemed linked to the diversity quotas imposed by the federal government, which forced companies to hire minority pilots, some with less than optimal skills.

But now, with the conversation's turn, Carlson brings up one such case to make a very different point. It involves a cargo pilot named Conrad Aska, who flew for Amazon contractor Atlas Air, whose Boeing 767 freighter crashed outside Houston in February 2019, killing him and the two others aboard. And, indeed, investigators would determine that pilot error had been the cause.

Tucker makes clear he doesn't blame Aska, who was "a nice guy trying to make his family proud," but "the guilty whites" who put him in the cockpit, adding "it was totally not his fault."

He pauses. "But leaving politics aside . . . there was a cockpit recorder, so we know his final thoughts, and it made me cry. This was a wonderful man. His last words, weren't 'Holy shit!' or, 'Mommy!' which is normal if you read transcripts of cockpit recorders, people crying out for their mothers when faced with death. Not me, I will not cry out for my mother." He laughs ruefully. "No, his last words, spoken calmly seconds before he hit the water at five hundred miles per hour were, 'Lord, you now have my soul.'

"When I read that I thought: I want to be that man. He'd studied for the exam — not the pilot's exam, he failed that one — but the life exam. If I'd known him, I would have asked 'How do you do that? How do you get to a place where staring death in the face through the cockpit window, that's what you feel?' Answering that question should be our national objective. Because that's the one thing that connects every human, the one unchanging fact, the certainty of death. You can change your political affiliation and all your ideas, you can pretend to change gender, but no matter what you do, it ends in death.

"So why don't we talk more about that — this finite life we all share, and its purpose? Why, for most of us today, is it so impolite to talk about, that if it's mentioned, it's usually batted down?"

"Because it is the basic fact that puts everything else in proper context, all vanity and stupidity people think are so important. There's daily human drama — this happens, that happens, this person takes power, these people get killed. But for each person it'll end the same way, which is alone and finally forced to deal with the questions we've been avoiding all these years — what happens next? It's your eighth-grade nightmare writ large. *What, the exam is right now? I never studied!*

"That's every person — the deep anxiety that rules people's lives. And most of us can't stop moving to avoid dealing with it."

Why does he think that is, I ask.

"It's because people today have decided they are God," he says, "and it's too horrible to raise questions that suggest otherwise. It suggests your insignificance in the natural order.

"If you acknowledge nature and its total independence from you — that it'll still be here when you're gone, trees will still be talking to each other — on some level that's really scary. If you look at the stars long enough, it will scare the shit out of you, because the main message is: you don't matter."

While a person of deep faith, Carlson does not flaunt his religion. "I'm an Episcopalian," he joked in a speech at the Heritage Foundation, "so don't take any theological advice from me, because I don't have any. I grew up in the shallowest faith tradition that's ever been invented. It's not even a Christian religion at this point."

Nonetheless, the subject comes up in various ways again and again, both in public settings and private conversation. Nature is wondrous, powerful, and inviolate, and humankind tampers with the natural order at great peril.

In a talk to the conservative youth group Turning Point USA, he got on the subject of how, in supposedly enlightened circles, everyone is expected to "pretend that men and women are exactly the same," which defies both the natural order and the whole of human experience. "They are not," said Carlson, "they are very different. And they need each other. They need each other. In order to be whole. That's the truth. They fit together like a jigsaw puzzle, physically and spiritually, for a reason, which is they complement each other. They need each other, *we* need each other. And anyone who tells you we don't is your enemy."

Of course, with the left having largely won on that front, and the most obvious and normal predilections of both sexes now routinely chalked up to social conditioning rather than nature, the ongoing war on biology has moved on to its current ferocious attack on the very existence of distinct sexes.

And, again, the word Carlson uses most often to characterize it is not some version of "crazy" or "appalling," though it is certainly both, "but evil."

Nor is there any question that, in his distress watching it take hold in the culture, he speaks for millions. "You all know what I'm talking about," as he put it to the audience at the Heritage Foundation, of the credulous and weak-willed who've allowed themselves to be bullied into subservience by zealots. "And you realize that the herd instinct is maybe the strongest instinct, maybe stronger than the hunger and sex instincts actually, the instinct, which again, is inherent to be like everybody else, and not to be cast out of the group, not to be shunned . . . it's harnessed by bad people in moments like this to produce uniformity. And you see people going along with this and you lose respect for them. And that's certainly happened to me at scale over the past three years. I'm not mad at people, I'm just sad and disappointed. How could you go along with this? You know it's not true, but you're saying it anyway. Really? You're putting your pronouns in your email? . . . What does that even mean? . . . You're saying things you can't define — LBGT and Q is a plus. Who's the plus? The plus is invited to my show anytime and I'll interview it on what it's like to be a plus. . . . Oh, shut up racist!"

But, he continued, "there is a countervailing force at work, always, there's a counterbalance to the badness — it's called goodness. And you see it in people. So for every ten people who are putting he/him in their electronic JP Morgan email signatures, there's one person who's 'No, I'm not doing that. Sorry, don't want to fight, but I'm not doing that. It's a betrayal of what I think is true, it's a betrayal of my conscience, of my faith, of my sense of myself, of my dignity as a human being, of my autonomy. I am not a slave, I am a free citizen, and I'm not doing that. And there's nothing you can do to me to make me do it. I hope it won't come to that. But if it does come to that, here I am, here I am. It's Paul on trial, 'Here I am.'

"You could not have known who these people are," he added meaningfully, "they don't fit a common profile. Some are people like me, some of them don't look like me at all. Some of them are people I despised on political grounds just a few years ago . . ." But "once you say one true thing and stick with it, all kinds of other true things occur to you. The truth is contagious — lying is, but the truth is, as well. And the second you decide to tell the truth about something you are filled with this, I don't wanna get supernatural on you, but you are filled with this power from somewhere else. Try it. Tell the truth about something, you feel it every day, the more you tell the truth, the stronger you become. That's completely real. It's measurable in the way that you feel. And, of course, the opposite is also true. The more you lie, the weaker and more terrified you become . . ."

So our road back, says Carlson, if there is to be one, must begin with truth telling, and if "you have people who are saying 'let's castrate the next generation, sexually mutilate children' — sorry, that's not a political debate. . . It's evil."

The Heritage speech, like my own many conversations with him, was discursive, often shifting tone and wandering where his restless mind took him, and it ran long, so at the end he good-naturedly apologized to his hosts. But in the end the pieces all fit together, and the sobering point, in its depth and meaning, was lost on no one.

Ironically — or maybe not — just three days after he delivered it, Fox gave him his walking papers.

AFTERMATH

Tucker Carlson is sitting in his small backyard on Florida's Gulf Coast smoking a cigar. It's been eight days since Fox News abruptly, and for reasons not yet clear, pulled the plug on his show.

"I'd say it's going pretty well," he tells me. "It's honestly the busiest time in my entire life. Everyone on staff, who I love, mostly quit or got fired — they all need jobs and I'm talking to them. I've got a lot of communication I'm going through, literally thousands of text messages I have to respond to. I'm still a Fox News employee, I'm still under contract. Obviously, I'd like that to end as quickly as possible."

He tells me the call came around eleven in the morning. He'd been up for hours and already filed his script for that night's monologue. In a supreme irony, it dealt with Alexandria Ocasio-Cortes's efforts to shut down his program, and the deadly threat such behavior by those in power poses to the nation's foundational principles. He was angry, and was really going to let her have it.

The phone rang. It was Fox News CEO Suzanne Scott. That day, April 24, was the six-year anniversary of *Tucker Carlson Tonight* moving into the prime 8:00 p.m. timeslot on the Fox News Channel, so Carlson thought the call was to congratulate him.

"I was first confused, and then shocked," he says. "It was just 'We're taking you off the air.' No explanation why, and they've let me guess ever since. That's literally all I know. I asked if I violated my contract. They said, no, I'm not fired, I'm still under contract."

He pauses. "Of course, the answer may just be that if enough people call for you to be canceled, ultimately you will be. The reaction was very bipartisan. The Pentagon celebrated when we got canceled. Republican leadership was pretty excited. Democrats were thrilled. I think if you don't have a really obvious team with power behind you, you get crushed, and that's probably what happened. But I don't know, there may be other reasons."

At exactly the same time, Tucker's executive producer Justin Wells was fielding a call from Fox executives Meade Cooper and Kevin Lord informing him that he, too, was out. It was a coordinated hit job.

I ask Carlson if he thinks his position on Ukraine may have had something to do with it, as was being widely speculated.

"The Murdochs definitely didn't like my views on Ukraine," he allows. "They told me that many times, both of them, to my face, 'we disagree with you on Ukraine.' Which is completely fine with me. They were big Zelenskyy people, or they felt they had to be, and I think Zelenskyy is a monster, and have said that many times, and I really mean it. But Lachlan came to my house for dinner in February of 2022, just him and me, when I was already under intense criticism for taking a different view of the war, it was really at fever pitch, and he told me: fine, you and I just disagree. Every time they said that

I had the same response, which was: I'm just so grateful that you let me disagree with you. Because it's one thing to employ someone who parrots your views, but it's a rare thing, it takes balls, to employ someone who attacks your views, and they get all the credit from me for that.

"So maybe it was over Ukraine, but I would be surprised, because they'd disagreed with me from the beginning, and from my perspective, the Murdochs were great about Ukraine."

While more upbeat than most might be in his situation, in Carlson's tone there is a certain weariness, even a hint of resignation. Having gotten to know him well over the past year, this is a side I have not seen. He is obviously drained.

But he's also defiant. "I have very high self-esteem," he adds a moment later, "and I don't feel bad about it because I know I didn't do anything wrong. Most bad things that happen to you are your fault. But it's not like I was caught sleeping with the makeup artist or I had to go to rehab. I've had a drinking problem; I've already beaten that."

"So I don't feel like I'd do anything differently. If you're drunk driving and you kill someone, that's a very different thing from shooting a home invader. In both cases you killed somebody. But if I killed someone [while] drunk driving, I don't think I'd ever sleep again; if I shot a home invader who was trying to hurt my kids, I'd sleep for eight hours."

Still, putting it mildly, he is disappointed in Fox. In an apparent freakout of epic proportions as the numbers in his old timeslot cratered disastrously in his absence, the network has responded with a campaign of slanders that might have come from the fever swamps of the left.

Even so, Tucker has not replied in kind, and has also told his allies to hold their fire. "I don't want to gloat about Fox in public," he tells me evenly. "I'm just way too close to it right now."

Two weeks later, things are starting to shake out. Though Tucker remains technically a Fox employee — just this morning he's received his usual paycheck from the network — speculation has been rife that he's lawyering up to take on News Corp for breach of contract, even as other reports have it that Fox is determined to hold him to the contract, and keep him off the air, through its end date — a month after the 2024 presidential election.

In any case, Tucker is no longer disposed to give Fox any benefit of the doubt. He's pissed, especially by how they've gone after him on the 'white men fight" text message.

"My view was you don't have to attack me, okay?" he says. "You cancelled my show, but that doesn't mean you have to tell people that you fired me — which they didn't; I'm still on the payroll as of right now. You don't have to attack me, because I don't deserve it. I didn't do anything wrong."

In fact, he says he now has a pretty good idea why, in seeming defiance of all logic, Fox did what it did. "They agreed to take me off the air, my show off the air, as a condition of the Dominion settlement. . . . They had to settle this; Rupert couldn't testify. I think that deal was made minutes before the trial started. I mean, I know it was."

Though Tucker doesn't say how he came by this bombshell, he delivers it with certainty.

He adds that he doesn't even take it personally, "because they had to. . . . But then Fox did start to attack me personally, which was uncalled for and unfair. Because I didn't do anything wrong."

Moreover, he says, while "if you read it literally it doesn't make any sense (because) I have nothing to do with the Dominion case at all," no one understands better that in today's distorted and deeply corrupt world, none of the old rules apply.

"I guess originally, the idea was to use my positions on the air as a way to help Dominion's case," he says, and "bolster their position that reasonable people should have known that Sidney Powell was lying. But that wasn't the purpose at all. The purpose was to emasculate Fox on the eve of a presidential election. Of course that was the point."

He adds that "we didn't make libelous claims. People came on and said things about Dominion. Well, all right. People come on TV and say things all the time. For two years people came on and said Donald Trump was a Russian agent . . . The whole claim was silly, and they got it in front of some sort of partisan, low-IQ jury, and they [Fox] were worried they were going to lose. So that's not justice, that's a scam. And the whole point was to emasculate Fox, take Fox out of the game but (because) Fox was a huge vector for Trumpism.

"That's what they thought, and they're right, and they didn't want that again.

"But from my point of view, I mean, this kind of thing happens all the time. It's a presidential election, it›s the biggest job in the world, people are not kidding about this, and why would they be?

People are willing to do a lot to influence who gets that job. And I understand that. I just felt annoyed that they were impugning my character in the process. But, whatever, I couldn't control it."

When it was announced this book was forthcoming, I received a letter from Dominion's attorney, that reads in part: "I wanted to make clear to you personally that Dominion made no demands or requests whatsoever regarding Mr. Carlson's employment with Fox or his appearance, or non-appearance, on Fox News, and as such no such conditions were agreed to—either in writing or verbally. Any suggestion otherwise is simply not true…In sum, whatever the reasons behind Fox's decision to take Mr. Carlson off the air, it cannot be blamed on any request or demand from Dominion."

Whatever the case, since the news broke of his cancellation, reports have had Carlson fielding offers from multiple other platforms, as well as from assorted extremely wealthy individuals. Even Fox, frantically scrambling to remake its primetime lineup to patch the yawning chasm in the middle, seems to have come to the belated realization that millions of viewers they thought were Fox fans were really Tucker fans all along.

"They'd lost some big talent before — they probably lost a few Boomers when O'Reilly left — but then Tucker brought in a completely different audience," says Wells. "I don't think they ever understood that it wasn't just a random cable-news show like Laura Ingraham or Chris Hayes; Tucker Carlson is a movement. I mean, you didn't just lose Harris Faulkner from *Outnumbered*. It's ridiculous that they don't understand the difference. But they really didn't realize what they had.

"They never realized that the Tucker brand was as substantial as theirs, and they could have catapulted it into its own, kind of the way that Oprah was such a big brand for CBS and eventually launched a channel around it."

Since Fox's canceling of his show, Tucker has made clear that he fully intends to not only keep doing what he does — speaking passionately about the vital issues that almost no one else in media will, or has the guts to — but, if possible, to do so for an even larger and more demographically diverse audience.

Nonetheless, his announcement that he's launching a new venture on Twitter — which he describes it as an even less constrained version of his Fox show — comes as a surprise, striking many on first hearing a significant comedown for Fox News's former reigning star; the network hadn't even bothered to forbid his becoming an online presence in his contract. But Wells stresses it will afford them the opportunity that, in its insular view, Fox failed to seize: a multidimensional platform built around Carlson's distinctive sensibility. "Twitter's relaunching their video platform as X Video, as a competitor to YouTube," he says, "so we're getting in on the early stages. We're looking at expanding into a large media company."

Moreover, Tucker himself now seems convinced that, body blow that his canceling was, it stands as stark proof of cable's inherent flaws and limitations — and that it was a good time to cut the cord.

"I really do think the cable-news business has a limited future," he tells me. "It's too obviously controlled. It's like Google — it's just become too clear that there's a certain selection of stories that are allowed, and a very thick file of stories that are *not* allowed. And I think people have come to understand that, and it's just not sustainable. I really think people are on to it, don't you? I see these clips of people on podcasts or just taking video of themselves on Twitter, and you can tell when someone's really telling the whole truth. It's obvious right away. Maybe I don't agree with the person, but I can see this person is not lying, he's saying what he really thinks, and that's immediately perceptible. You can tell when someone's lying to you or when someone's shading the truth or trying to spin you. And there's a lot of artifice in television."

Supposedly no-longer-leftist CNN covered the news of Tucker's move to Twitter this way: "Right-wing extremist Tucker Carlson announced Tuesday that he will relaunch his program on Twitter, which he praised as the only remaining large free-speech platform in the world after Fox News fired him late last month."

Fox News — which I've been told has banned any mention of Tucker's name on air — did not cover it at all.

All of which fits perfectly with the reasons Tucker laid out — in his announcement on Twitter, laced with clear elements of autobiography — for why his new venture is needed. It is, he said, because the news media, without exception, mislead us as a matter of course "in every story that matters, every day of the week, every week of the year. What's it like to work in a system like that? After thirty years in the middle of it, we could tell you stories. The best you can hope for in the news business at this point is to tell the fullest truth that you can. But there are always limits. And you know that if you keep bumping up against those limits often enough you will be fired for it. That's not a guess — it's a guarantee. Every person who works in English-language media understands that. The rule of what you *can't* say defines everything. It's filthy, really. And it's utterly corrupting. You can't have a free society if people aren't allowed to say what they think is true. Speech is the fundamental prerequisite for democracy . . ."

Now, at last, in this new venue, he would be his own boss, without constraints.

Tucker Carlson unbound?

Already there were millions waiting to see what *that* would look like.

ACKNOWLEDGEMENTS

This book would not have been possible without the hard work and guidance of my editor, Harry Stein, a brilliant and extremely talented man who I'm honored to consider a friend.

Equally, I extend my deepest gratitude to everyone at All Seasons Press, and especially Gray Delany, for the conviction and dedication they put toward this project.

My research assistant, Mitchell Sances, continues to be among the brightest, best, and most reliable around and it's such a pleasure to know and work with him.

Tucker and Susie Carlson welcomed me into their home and their lives with incomparable warmth and generosity. They reminded me of the things that truly matter in life—love, dogs, and the stars— and for that I will be forever grateful.

As with Dick Carlson, whose fascinating and colorful life deserves a book of its own.

I'd also like to thank everyone at Media Matters for America and their affiliated sectarian drones in mainstream media who, despite dedicating countless hours and entire assassination squads in the service of taking out Tucker Carlson, ran and hid under the covers whenever asked for an interview. Your insincerity and cowardice remain on full display for anyone paying the least amount of attention. Thank you for being so hideous and stupid.

And, finally, for Nate—my best friend and partner in life, a man I admire more than any other. I love you.